GUINNESS WORLD RECORDS

Funky Foods

by Nancy Bosse and Shirley Pearson

Carson-Dellosa Publishing LLC
Greensboro, North Carolina

Credits

Content Editor: Christine Schwab

Copy Editor: Julie B. Killian

Layout and Cover Design: Van Harris

Carson-Dellosa Publishing LLC
PO Box 35665
Greensboro, NC 27425 USA
www.carsondellosa.com

ISBN 9781609964641
01-335111151

TABLE OF CONTENTS

Setting Guinness World Records Records.........4

Be a Record Breaker! 5

The Real Everlasting Gobstopper? 6

No Licking Allowed 7

One Grain at a Time 8

Fudge Frenzy 9

The Top Banana 10

A Record with a Twist 11

Snacking on Sprouts 12

A Staggering Stack of Flapjacks 14

Pizza Party 15

How Sweet It Is! 16

Where Did This Egg Come From? 17

Hamburger Lineup 18

Snail Smorgasbord 19

A Pool of Pasta................................20

Gingerbread Giant 21

Flying Ice Cream 22

For the Love of Pizza 24

Get It While It's Hot! 25

Feel the Heat 26

Potatoes Au Giant 27

An Eggs-ellent Omelet.........................28

Meatball Muncher 29

The Boat That Didn't Float......................30

It's in the Bag! 31

For Big Appetites Only 32

A Ton of Cereal...............................33

Dessert Rink 34

Mama Tamale 35

A Monster-Sized Matzo Ball 36

What a Classy Dog! 37

This Record Takes the Cake! 38

He Is Stuffed! 39

Let Them Eat Cake............................40

Chocolate-Lovers' Delight 41

Onion Energy 42

Juice Jumping 43

Salad on the Menu 44

A Towering Record............................46

Please Pass the Pasta 47

Paella for a Crowd 48

Anniversary Kiss.............................49

No Loafing Here!.............................50

Two Pies Each...............................51

King of the Burgers 52

Mounds and Mounds of Meatballs.................53

Gooey Goodies 54

Rocket Man..................................55

Caution! Pizza Crossing.......................56

It's Delish! 57

One Potato, Two Potato 58

The Wall Against Hunger.......................59

Fans Flipping Flapjacks 60

Big Mac, Please 61

Try Catching This Ball! 62

Soup's On! 64

How Many Pieces Do You Wish? 65

Egg-stravaganza 66

A Mammoth Marshmallow Muffin 67

A Refreshing Record 68

Curry for a Cause 69

Big Boil and Bake 70

Cupcake or "Tubcake"?........................71

Pizza Acrobat................................72

Sweet Jar of Jelly Beans.......................73

Stacker Packer Power 74

Say Cheesecake!.............................75

A Record to Float Your Boat! 76

Jumbo Shrimp? 77

Tons of Tea..................................78

Smooth Move! 79

Great Grapes at the Grand Canyon.................80

Want a Piece of the Pie? 82

That Is Using Your Noodle 83

Chocolate Church 84

Let It Roll! 85

Ah, So Sweet! 86

What a Spread! 88

Save a Bite for Me! 89

One Humongous Hotcake 90

Long Line of Lolly Lovers 91

Biggest, Bar None! 92

Tasty Test...................................93

Answer Key..................................94

SETTING GUINNESS WORLD RECORDS RECORDS

Guinness World Records accomplishments are facts or events that belong in one of eight categories:

- Human Body
- Amazing Feats
- Natural World
- Science and Technology
- Arts and Media
- Modern Technology
- Travel and Transport
- Sports and Games

Some records are new because they are exciting and involve events that have never been attempted before. People with unique talents or features are also permitted to become record setters. However, many of the records are already established, and people try to find records that they can break. One record holder, Ashrita Furman, has broken or set more than 300 records since 1979.

Guinness World Records receives more than 60,000 requests each year. Record setters and breakers must apply first so that their attempts are official. The organization sets guidelines for each event to make sure that it can be properly measured. Guinness World Records also makes sure that all record breakers follow the same steps so that each participant gets an equal chance. Professional judges make sure that the guidelines are followed correctly and measured accurately. However, the guidelines may designate other community members who can serve as judges to witness an event. Once the record attempt is approved, the participant gets a framed certificate. The person's name may also be included in the yearly publication or on the Guinness World Records Web site at *www.guinnessworldrecords.com*.

BE A RECORD BREAKER!

Hey, kids!

Tubby is a Labrador retriever that collected and recycled about 26,000 plastic bottles from his daily walks. Rob Williams (USA) made a sandwich with his feet in less than two minutes. Tiana Walton (UK) placed 27 gloves on one hand at one time. Aaron Fotheringham (USA) landed the first wheelchair backflip. The Heaviest Pumpkin ever weighed 1,725 pounds (782.45 kg). And Rosi, the Heaviest Spider ever, is larger than a dinner plate. What do all of these stories have in common? They are Guinness World Records records!

A world record is an amazing achievement that is a fact. It can be a skill someone has, such as being able to blow the largest bubble gum bubble. It can be an interesting fact from nature, such as which bird is the smelliest bird. Guinness World Records has judges who set rules to make sure that all record setters and record breakers follow the same steps. Then, the adjudicators (judges) count, weigh, measure, or compare to make sure that the achievement is the greatest in the world.

So, can you be a Guinness World Records record breaker? If you can run, hop, toss, or even race with an egg on a spoon, you just might see your name on a Guinness World Records Certificate someday. With the help of an adult, visit *www.guinnessworldrecords.com*. There you will find a world of exciting records to explore—and maybe break!

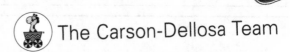 The Carson-Dellosa Team

The Real Everlasting Gobstopper?

Largest Jawbreaker
May 29, 2003

A jawbreaker (also called a gobstopper) is a hard, round candy. You don't chew a jawbreaker. You suck on it, for a long time! Have you ever read Roald Dahl's book *Charlie and the Chocolate Factory*? Or, have you seen the related movie about Charlie and the candy maker Willy Wonka? If you have, then you know that Mr. Wonka invented a jawbreaker called "the Everlasting Gobstopper." Could a candy like that really last forever? It probably could not. But in 2003, real-life candy maker Nick Calderaro (Canada) created a jawbreaker so big that it could have come straight from Mr. Wonka's fictional factory. The giant jawbreaker weighed 27.8 pounds (12.6 kg), which is about the weight of a one-year-old child! With a circumference of 37.25 inches (94.6 cm), the record-setting jawbreaker could really challenge any jaw! Calderaro, an employee of Oak Leaf Confections, spent 476 hours over a four-and-a-half-month period making this single piece of candy.

● Using the clues below, create two-word phrases that rhyme with *jawbreaker* and *gobstopper*. The first word in each two-word phrase rhymes with *jaw* or *gob*; the second word in each phrase rhymes with *breaker* or *stopper*. The first one has been done for you.

Jawbreaker Rhymes	
1. **r a w b a k e r**	A type of **cook** who only uses **uncooked** food.
2. ___ ___ ___ ___ ___ ___ ___ ___	An animal that **gathers leaves** using **long fingernails**.
3. ___ ___ ___ ___ ___ ___ ___ ___ ___	Someone who **shakes** an **animal's hand**.
Gobstopper Rhymes	
4. ___ ___ ___ ___ ___ ___ ___ ___ ___ ___	Someone who **cuts up** an **ear of corn**.
5. ___ ___ ___ ___ ___ ___ ___ ___ ___	Someone who **jumps** around at **work**.
6. ___ ___ ___ ___ ___ ___ ___ ___ ___ ___ ___	A **messy person** who loves to **buy stuff**.

No Licking Allowed

Most Jelly Doughnuts Eaten in Three Minutes
May 2, 2007

The record for the Most Jelly Doughnuts Eaten in Three Minutes is six. Six doughnuts may not sound like very many. That is about 30 seconds per doughnut. But, before you start boasting that you could break that record, you should know a key requirement. Remember they are coated in sugar! You must complete this feat without licking your lips. That's right, no licking! It is not as easy as it sounds. Lup Fun Yau (UK) tied the record set by Steve McHugh (UK) in 2004. Does Yau have incredible self-control? Or, does he not find jelly doughnuts lip-lickingly delicious? Either way, he got his name in the *Guinness World Records* book.

● Using each number only once, write the numbers 1, 2, 3, 4, 5, and 6 so that the sum of each row of **three** doughnuts, across and down, equals the number in the box.

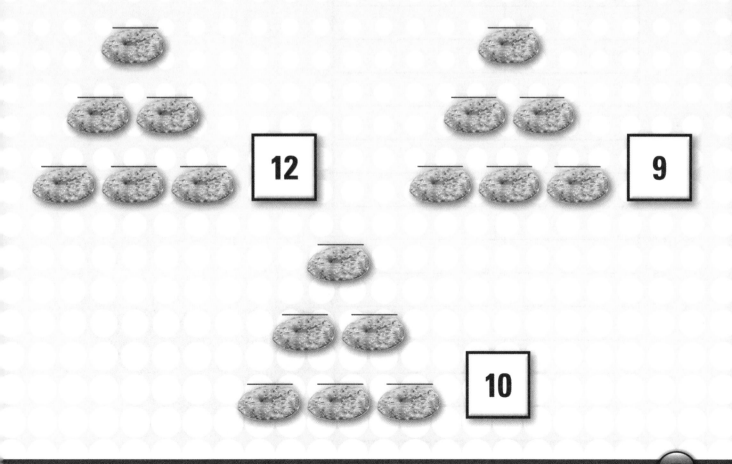

One Grain at a Time

Most Rice Eaten in Three Minutes
November 9, 2007

Some people use chopsticks to eat their meals. However, if you are not used to using chopsticks, they can be a little tricky to work. Rob Beaton (USA) used chopsticks to set a record. He set the record for the Most Rice Eaten in Three Minutes. He ate 78 grains of rice. That might seem too simple. But, Beaton ate the rice one grain at a time. He picked up each tiny grain of rice using chopsticks. Even if you are used to using chopsticks, picking up one grain of rice can be a challenge. Just imagine how much sticky rice Beaton could scoop into his mouth in three minutes!

● Rob Beaton ate 78 grains of rice in three minutes. Complete the chart to figure out how long it would take him to eat more than 1,000 grains of rice if he continued at this rate.

Minutes	Grains of Rice
3	78
6	156
9	234

Fudge Frenzy

Largest Slab of Fudge
June 29, 2009

You can buy fudge in a one-pound (453 g) slab, but you probably only eat a small piece of it at a time. Fudge is so sweet that any more might give you a stomachache. The slab of fudge that William "Chef Nick" Nicklosovich and "Peppermint Jim" Crosby (USA) made in 2009 at Lansing Community College was a lot bigger than a normal slab of fudge. Half was chocolate. The other half was mint chocolate. The entire slab weighed 5,200 pounds (2.35 tonnes)! Chef Nick and Peppermint Jim, along with dozens of students, worked on the fudge for three days. Volunteers walked across wooden platforms while pouring the fudge mixture into a gigantic wooden tray. The slab measured 36.25 feet (11 m) by 8.25 feet (2.5 m). And, at 8 inches (20.3 cm) high, you wouldn't be able to sink your teeth into much of it. But, the good thing was that you didn't have to. After being weighed for the world record, the Largest Slab of Fudge was cut into normal-sized pieces and sold. Proceeds from the sale went to charity.

Word Bank					
cake	fudge	lemon	mint	roll	tart

● *Fudge* and *mint* are words that name foods. These words also have other meanings. Read the following sentences. The underlined word in each sentence describes the missing food word but in a different way. Write the correct word from the word bank beside each sentence.

1. If you <u>fake</u> your answers on the test, you will probably do poorly. _____ _____ _____ _____ _____

2. The United States used to <u>make metal coins</u> pennies out of copper. _____ _____ _____ _____

3. That mud will <u>harden</u> on your boots if you don't wash it off. _____ _____ _____

4. If you <u>turn</u> over, you will fall off the couch. _____ _____ _____ _____

5. This new car has broken down again! It must be a <u>defective car</u>. _____ _____ _____

6. She spoke in such a <u>sharp</u> voice that my little brother started to cry. _____ _____ _____ _____

Largest Collection of Banana-Related Memorabilia
February 12, 1999

Ken Bannister (USA) is bananas about bananas! He started collecting banana-related things more than 30 years ago. He has the largest collection in the world. His collection includes plastic bananas, stuffed bananas, banana mugs, banana soaps, banana clocks, banana puppets—you name it. If it looks like a banana, it is probably in Bannister's collection. He has even been seen wearing a banana jumpsuit and banana slippers!

Bannister displays his banana collection at his International Banana Club Museum in California. The museum shows off more than 17,000 banana-related items. Bannister received many of these items from his fans and club members. The club has more than 9,000 members from 27 countries. Bannister likes to say they are a really fun "bunch"!

● Below are 10 of Bannister's bananas in an upside-down triangle. Find a way to move only three bananas so that the triangle is right-side up. Draw the new stack of bananas.

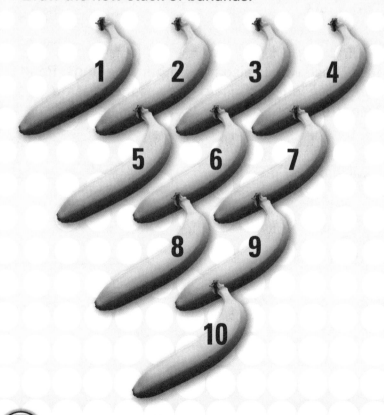

A Record with a Twist

Largest Pretzel
September 21, 2008

Here is a twist on a popular snack: the world's Largest Pretzel. Olaf Kluy and Manfred Keilwerth (both Germany) made this amazing twisted snack. It weighed 842 pounds (382 kg) and measured 26 feet 10 inches (8.2 m) long. It was also 10 feet 2 inches (3.1 m) wide.

Pretzels were first made using scraps of dough left over when baking bread. The scraps were twisted, baked, and salted. Then, the scraps were handed out to the poor. Imagine how many people this giant pretzel could feed!

● Use the grid to help you solve the riddle. Write the matching letter for each ordered pair.

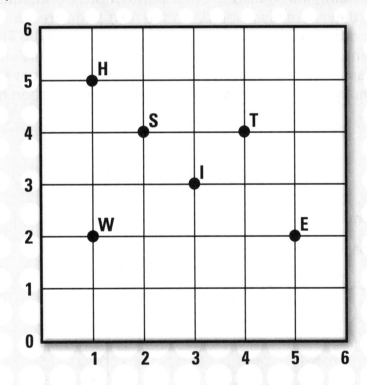

What is a pretzel's favorite dance?

___ ___ ___ ___ ___ ___ ___ ___
(4,4) (1,5) (5,2) (4,4) (1,2) (3,3) (2,4) (4,4)

Most Brussels Sprouts Eaten in One Minute
November 26, 2008

Brussels sprouts are small, round vegetables that are packed with nutrients. They look like tiny cabbages, and they are delicious. But, a lot of people think they don't like Brussels sprouts. Fireman Linus Urbanec (Sweden) isn't one of those people. In just one minute, Urbanec ate 31 of these vitamin-packed veggies. Guinness World Records rules stated that the sprouts had to be at least 2.5 inches (6.4 cm) in diameter and had to be eaten one at a time using a toothpick. Urbanec followed the rules and set a new world record.

● Brussels is the capital of the European country of Belgium. Brussels sprouts first became popular there before being introduced to other parts of the world. Many foods are named for the places where they were discovered. On the next page are some food samples. The foods are named for different cities or towns throughout the world. The city portions of the names are written vertically down the toothpicks; the food portions of the names are written horizontally across the food samples. The words intersect at a common letter. Using the clues, complete the missing words. The first one has been done for you.

1. (Brussels, Belgium)

A small, round cabbage-like vegetable

Brussels s p r o u t

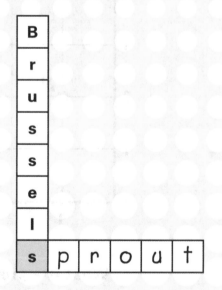

2. (Cheddar, UK)

This is a common pizza topping made from milk. It is also used on a grilled sandwich and as a hamburger topping.

```
          C
          h
☐ ☐ ☐ e ☐ ☐
          d
          d
          a
          r
```

Cheddar ___ ___ ___ ___ ___ ___ ___

3. (Valencia, Spain)

This round, juicy fruit is also the name of a color. This fruit's juice is a common breakfast drink.

```
          V
          a
          l
          e
          n
          c
          i
☐ ☐ a ☐ ☐ ☐
```

Valencia ___ ___ ___ ___ ___ ___ ___

4. (Rome, USA)

Eating one of these fruits every day is said to keep the doctor away.

```
          R
          o
          m
☐ ☐ ☐ ☐ e
```

Rome ___ ___ ___ ___

5. (Vidalia, USA)

You might cry when cutting into the layers of this white vegetable.

```
          V
          i
          d
          a
          l
☐ ☐ i ☐ ☐
          a
```

Vidalia ___ ___ ___ ___ ___

CD-104547

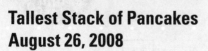
A Staggering Stack of Flapjacks

GUINNESS WORLD RECORDS

Tallest Stack of Pancakes
August 26, 2008

You may want to grab some syrup and a fork when you read about this record breaker: the world's Tallest Stack of Pancakes. Some restaurants serve a short stack of pancakes. A short stack is usually made up of two or three pancakes. This record-breaking stack was not a short stack. It had 672 pancakes! Each pancake was between 9 and 10 inches (23 and 25 cm) wide. The stack measured 2 feet 5 inches (74 cm) high. Krunoslav Budiselic (Croatia) made the pancake tower. It took him 22 hours to complete.

● Lincoln Elementary had a pancake breakfast. Participants sold the same number of pancakes as the number of pancakes in the Tallest Stack of Pancakes. Look at the graph. Figure out how many banana nut pancakes were sold. Complete the graph.

Pancakes Sold at the Lincoln Elementary Pancake Breakfast

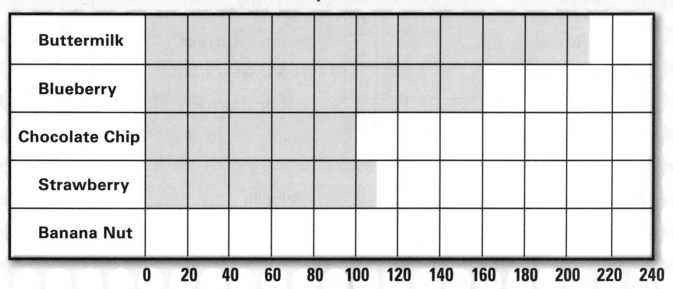

At the breakfast, _____ banana nut pancakes were sold.

CD-104547

Pizza Party

Longest Line of Pizzas
May 16, 2009

What do you call almost 2,000 pizzas lined up, side by side, creating the Longest Line of Pizzas in the world? It's a pizza party! In May 2009, the Van Duzer Foundation and the St. Lucie County Education Foundation (USA) decided to take on the Longest Line of Pizzas record. They were successful. How long was that record line of 12-inch (30.5 cm) pizzas? It was 1,777 feet 10 inches (541.8 m), which is about the length of two football fields. The Van Duzer family owns the local pizza shop that baked all of the pizzas. They also created the Van Duzer Foundation, which helps local families deal with tragedy. The Van Duzers

"cooked up" the idea of trying for the record. A dozen volunteers began preparations and cooking three days before the event. And, it took 750 student volunteers to create the giant pizza line. What happened to those 6,000 slices of pizza? They were eaten, of course, at no charge!

● Below are six different kinds of pizzas. Using the clues, label the pizzas with the correct pizza labels.

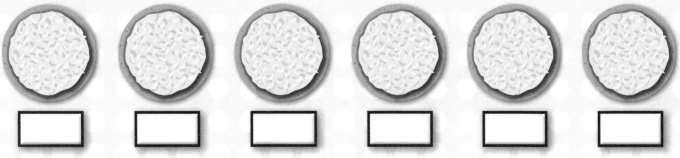

Pizza Label	Kind of Pizza
A	pepperoni
B	cheese
C	pineapple and ham
D	sausage and mushroom
E	vegetarian
F	extra cheese

Clues

The vegetarian pizza is the last pizza.

The pizza with ham is the second pizza.

The pizza with mushrooms is beside the vegetarian pizza.

The pizza with extra cheese is beside the pizza with pineapple.

The cheese pizzas are side by side.

Largest Candy Mosaic
October 18, 2009

Have you ever made a mosaic? Perhaps you used colored eggshells or paper scraps. The little pieces blend together to make one picture. This record-breaking mosaic was pretty sweet! It set the record for the Largest Candy Mosaic. It was 30 feet 2 inches (9.2 m) high and 28 feet 3 inches (8.6 m) wide. That is about the same size as 18 ping-pong tables grouped in three rows of six tables. The mosaic was made up of 150,000 Sugus candies. Sugus are small square candies made by the Wrigley Company in Spain. More than 1,200 children helped create the mosaic. It took three days to create. Later it was sold. The money was used to help children with cancer.

● **Sugus candies come in several colors including yellow (Y), orange (O), red (R), purple (P), and blue (B). Look at the patterns. Answer the questions.**

1. What color would the 10ᵗʰ candy in this pattern be? _____

2. What color would the 20ᵗʰ candy in this pattern be? _____

3. What color would the 14ᵗʰ candy in this pattern be? _____

4. What color would the 40ᵗʰ candy in this pattern be? _____

Where Did This Egg Come From?

Largest Scotch Egg
September 7, 2008

● Fill in the missing letters to complete the passage. Then use the letters to complete the puzzle below.

The world's Largest Scotch Egg weighed 13.6 pounds (6.2 kg). It w___s "laid" on a plate on July 30, 2008. Chef Lee Streeton (UK) cooked the dish. He began with just o___e egg from the specialty egg producer Clarence Court. Was this breakfast fo___d really made from an egg that big? No, it was not! The original egg weighed 3.7 pound___ (1.7 kg), which is equal to two-and-a-half dozen chicken eggs. The res___ of the "Scotch egg" was sausage meat (8.8 pounds; 4 kg), haggis (2.06 pounds; 940 g), and bread c___umbs (1.75 pounds; 800 g).

A Scotch egg ___s an ordinary hard-boiled egg wrapped in meat, ___overed in bread crumbs, and fried. It is a popular breakfast food in the United Kingdom. This record-setting Scotch egg included haggis. ___aggis is a traditional Scottish food mad___ from sheep or calf organs. But, the real star in this massive Scotch e___g was the egg. Just boilin___ this egg took one-and-a-half hours!

The missing letters in the passage above spell, in order,
the kind of egg that Chef Streeton used.

___ ___ ___ ___ ___ ___ ___ ___ ___ ___ ___

CD-104547

Hamburger Lineup

Longest Line of Hamburgers
May 30, 2009

This lineup is not a baseball batting order. It is the Longest Line of Hamburgers. The incredible lineup of hamburgers measured 1,004 feet 10 inches (306 m). Workers from the Kuwait Food Company Americana (Kuwait) lined up 2,500 hamburgers to set the record. The hamburgers were from Hardee's, one of the company's restaurant chains. The hamburger lineup was just one part of an exciting day of food and fun. Over 500 employees from the company participated to help break two other records that same day! One was for the Largest Bucket of Kentucky Fried Chicken, and the other was for the Largest Box of Krispy Kreme Doughnuts. Participants arranged the doughnuts to look like one of the Kuwait Towers. What a day filled with tasty fun!

● Find the numbers on the hamburgers that add up to the number on the right. Start with the number in the bottom-left corner. End at the number in the bottom-right corner. The added numbers must be next to each other—above, beside, or below.

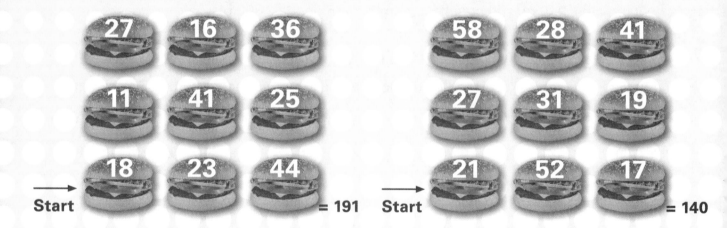

27	16	36		58	28	41
11	41	25		27	31	19
18	23	44		21	52	17

Start ... = 191   Start ... = 140

CD-104547

Snail Smorgasbord

Largest Serving of Snails
July 11, 2009

Every summer, the city of Loures, Portugal, puts on a *Festival do Caracol*. For two weeks, thousands of tourists crowd Loures's restaurants. The tourists come to eat a tasty spiral-shelled seafood called caracol, which is Portuguese for "snail." Thousands of pounds of these creatures are served up during the festival each year. In 2009, the Loures City Council set a new world record for the Largest Serving of Snails. The council cooked 2,449 pounds (1,111 kg) of caracol and served them in a single dish. The cooking pot was so big that it needed six burners to heat it up.

● Boiling snails is one way to cook them. But, during the Festival do Caracol, chefs experiment with much fancier dishes. Listed below are the incomplete names of eight snail dishes. The missing letters can be found in the snail eyes, which are located on top of the snails' antennae. Complete the snail dish names. The missing letters, in order, will spell the French word that chefs everywhere use for snails.

___ ___ ___ ___ ___ ___ ___ ___

Menu
Bak____d Snails
Snail Pa____ta
____reamed Snails
Snail Pizz____
F____ied Snails
____rilled Snails
Snail S ____up
Snail S____ew

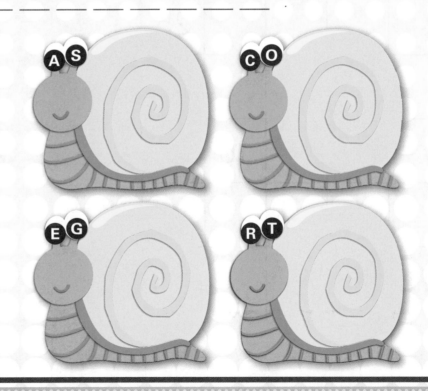

A Pool of Pasta

Largest Bowl of Pasta
March 12, 2010

If you had jumped into this pool, you would have wanted to bring a fork. The swimming pool was filled with spaghetti noodles! This pool of noodles set the record for the Largest Bowl of Pasta, weighing in at 13,786 pounds (6,253 kg). The owner of the Buca di Beppo Italian Restaurant (USA) wanted to set a new record, and he did it. He beat the previous record by more than 4,000 pounds! It took five people 120 hours to cook the pasta. Then, a team lined up in a "bucket brigade" to pour all of the noodles into the pool. To top it off, the team added 120 gallons (38 L) of tomato sauce to the pasta. The record was achieved! None of the pasta went to waste. It was donated and reused by the local farming community.

- Numbering as you go, draw one continuous piece of cooked spaghetti so that it touches each box in the 5 by 5 grid. Start at 1 and end at 25. The pasta must go through the boxes with numbers in order. Number the boxes to show the path of the pasta.

				25
	1			
			16	
11				

Gingerbread Giant

Largest Gingerbread Man
September 11, 2009

The gingerbread man in the folktale bragged about being fast. But, this gingerbread man could have bragged about being big! The giant cookie broke the record for the Largest Gingerbread Man. It weighed 1,435 pounds 3 ounces (651 kg). That is one big cookie! The gingerbread man that held the record before weighed 1,308 pounds 8 ounces (6.1 kg). But, the IKEA store in Oslo, Norway, decided to make an even bigger cookie. They baked it in one piece at a local bakery. Sultan Koesen (Turkey) unveiled the big cookie. Koesen was the perfect man for the job. At 8 feet 1 inch (246.3 cm) tall, he had already set his own record, the record for being the world's Tallest Man.

● Anna, Jayden, Cole, and Iesha decorated gingerbread men. Read the clues to find out who decorated which gingerbread man. Then, write the name under each child's cookie.

Anna's cookie is next to the cookie with an odd number of buttons.

One girl's cookie has stripes instead of squiggles.

One boy's cookie has a vest.

Jayden added more details to his cookie than Cole.

_____   _____   _____   _____

Flying Ice Cream

Most Ice-Cream Scoops Thrown and Caught in One Minute by a Team of Two
September 1, 2007

When Gabriele Soravia and his son, Lorenzo (both Germany), stepped onto a TV show's stage in Cologne, Germany, they saw that the audience was wearing plastic raincoats. The TV show was for Guinness World Records attempts, and the Soravias were there to try for the record in ice-cream throwing. Luckily for the audience, the Soravias were throwing the ice cream at each other. And even luckier, their aim was pretty good! The Soravias walked away with a new record: the Most Ice-Cream Scoops Thrown and Caught in One Minute by a Team of Two. Gabriele was the thrower. He had to dig out a scoop of ice cream and toss it toward his son. Lorenzo was the catcher, standing about 26 feet (8 m) away. For each throw, Lorenzo had to grab an empty cone and catch the flying ball of ice cream. Some ice cream landed on Lorenzo. Some ice cream landed on the floor. But, no ice cream ended up on the audience's plastic raincoats. So, what was the new world record? The Soravias managed to put together 25 flying ice-cream cones in just a single minute.

● On the next page are eight balls of ice cream. Each ball contains a letter. The thrower is trying to land each ball of ice cream into one of three ice-cream cones. The cones contain words, but each word is missing a letter. The catcher has to decide which of the three cones to use for each ice-cream ball thrown. The ice-cream letters must fit into the blank spaces in the cone words. The completed words also must have something to do with the Soravias' world record. For each ball of ice cream, complete the correct cone word and circle the ice-cream cone.

Each ice-cream cone has a pair of letters below it. Look at your circled cones. In order from top to bottom, write the correct pairs of letters in the spaces below. The letters will spell the type of family business that the Soravia family owns.

___ ___   ___ ___ ___-___ ___ ___ ___   ___ ___ ___ ___ ___

CD-104547

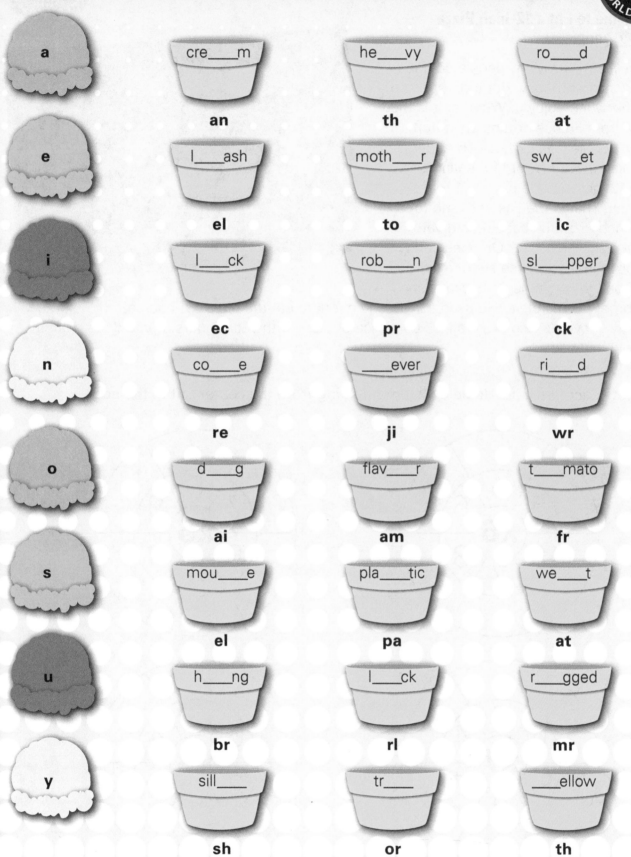

a

e

i

n

o

s

u

y

cre___m	he___vy	ro___d
an	**th**	**at**
l___ash	moth___r	sw___et
el	**to**	**ic**
l___ck	rob___n	sl___pper
ec	**pr**	**ck**
co___e	___ever	ri___d
re	**ji**	**wr**
d___g	flav___r	t___mato
ai	**am**	**fr**
mou___e	pla___tic	we___t
el	**pa**	**at**
h___ng	l___ck	r___gged
br	**rl**	**mr**
sill___	tr___	___ellow
sh	**or**	**th**

CD-104547

For the Love of Pizza

Fastest Time to Eat a 12-Inch Pizza
March 22, 2008

Do you like pizza? Many people do. Pizza may have started in Italy. But today, people all over the world enjoy it. Whether it is fried-egg pizza from France or tuna pizza from Germany, people love pizza. Josh Anderson (New Zealand) set a record for eating pizza. He ate a 12-inch cheese pizza in 1 minute, 45 seconds. That is the Fastest Time to Eat a 12-Inch Pizza. Is that a record you could sink your teeth into? Or, does eating a 12-inch pizza in record time seem a bit rude to you? Don't worry, though, because Josh did not forget his manners. He used a knife and a fork to eat the pizza. Of course, you already know it's also okay to pick up a slice of pizza with your fingers. If you don't want it to drip, fold it in half!

● Complete each pizza puzzle below by multiplying from the center out to the edge.

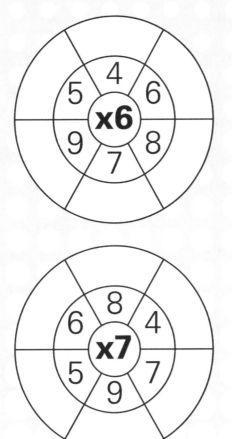

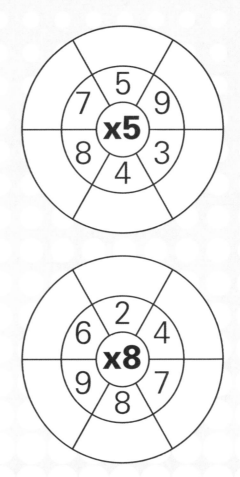

Get It While It's Hot!

Largest Hot Cross Bun
April 4, 2009

"Hot cross buns, hot cross buns, one a penny, two a penny, hot cross buns . . ." This record is no nursery rhyme! It is the world's Largest Hot Cross Bun. Workers at Safari Dried Fruit and Sasko Bakeries (both South Africa) made the gigantic bun. It weighed 227 pounds (103 kg). That is about the same weight as 1,300 regular-sized hot cross buns. Workers had to use a special pan to bake this oversized bun. The pan was almost 6 feet (1.8 m) in diameter.

Hot cross buns are made from dough that includes nutmeg, cinnamon, and raisins. After baking, the buns are decorated with a frosting cross. The record-setting bun did not go to waste. It was taken to the Red Cross Children's Hospital where the young patients enjoyed the tasty treat.

● Write numbers on the four corners of the hot cross buns below that, when multiplied across and down, equal the numbers to the right and below the buns. The first one has been done for you.

2	9	18
4	5	20
8	45	

		42
		21
18	49	

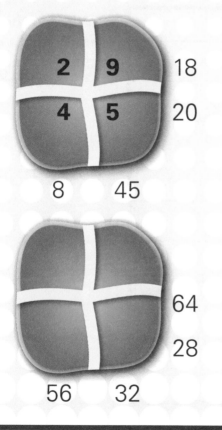

		64
		28
56	32	

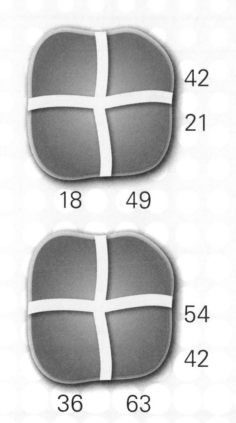

		54
		42
36	63	

Most Jalapeño Peppers Eaten in One Minute
September 17, 2006

What gives a bowl of chili or salsa its spicy taste? It's the peppers! One of the spiciest peppers is a long, skinny pepper called a jalapeño. Jalapeños are surprisingly nutritious. They are a great source of vitamins A and C, as well as potassium. But, eating jalapeños to help stay healthy is tricky. That's because jalapeño peppers are hot! Eating just one can burn your mouth. Just ask Alfredo Hernandes (USA). He holds the record for the Most Jalapeño Peppers Eaten in One Minute. In 2006, Hernandes took part in a local restaurant's Feel the Heat Challenge. In just one minute, he ate 16 3-inch-long (7.6 cm) jalapeños. Doesn't that make you break out in a sweat just to imagine such a feat?

● Listed below are some other "hot" foods. These foods aren't spicy like jalapeño peppers. They're hot because they contain the letters **h**, **o**, and **t**. Using the clues, fill in the missing **hot** letters. The circled letters, in order, will spell the answer to this question:

Food	Clues
Ⓙelly d__ug__nu__	baked treat with a hole in the middle
sm__o__ __ie	thick fruity drink
c__t__@ge c__eese	chunky dairy product
c__oc__Ⓛa__e	sweet brown candy
c__erry t__ma__o	small, round red fruit
t__@s__	breakfast food
Ⓟis__ac__i__	nuts with dyed red shells
ar__ic__ __ke	green vegetable with a "heart"
s __ __r__bre@d	sweet holiday cookie

What is the name of the Mexican city where jalapeño peppers were first grown?

—— —— —— —— —— —— —— ——

Potatoes Au Giant

Largest Potato Gratin
January 29, 2010

The basic recipe for a potato gratin is simple. Cut the potatoes. Add cream. Bake. That does not sound too difficult, unless you want to set the record for the Largest Potato Gratin. The people at l'Office du Tourisme in Alpe d'Huez, France, did just that. First, they cut 2,700 potatoes. Then, they added 661.39 pounds (300 kg) of cream. They also added 22.05 pounds (10 kg) of garlic. They poured the mixture onto a special cooking surface that measured about 33 feet (10 m) by 6 feet (2 m). That is about the same size as 10 twin-sized mattresses grouped in two rows of five mattresses each. The workers used boat oars to stir the gratin as it cooked. In the end, this record breaker weighed almost 6,636 pounds (3,010 kg). It looked like a winner and tasted like one too!

- Six children sat in a circle to play hot potato. In this particular game, the fifth person that touches the hot potato is out. The potato starts with Riley and must be passed clockwise. No child can be skipped. After several rounds of play, which child will be sitting in the circle?

CD-104547

An Eggs-ellent Omelet

Largest Omelet
October 8, 2010

This record may crack you up! It took 110,000 cracked eggs! That is how many eggs went into the world's Largest Omelet. The omelet weighed 9,702 pounds 8 ounces (4.4 tonnes). That weight beat the previous record by 2,000 pounds. Yum-Bir (the Turkish Egg Producers Association) and the Pruva Neta tourist agency (both Turkey) set the record. The record-breaking event was part of the celebration of World Egg Day. It took the head chef and a team of 60 other chefs more than two hours to prepare the omelet for cooking. Then, they cooked it in a pan almost 33 feet (10 m) wide. It took more than two hours to cook this breakfast treat. And, the omelet turned out eggs-ellent!

● Lisa, Michael, and Chase ordered different omelets for breakfast. One ordered a plain cheese omelet, one ordered a ham and cheese omelet, and one ordered a bacon and Swiss cheese omelet. They also ordered different types of drinks. Read the clues and mark the chart to figure out who ordered which omelet and which drink.

The child who ordered the plain cheese omelet did not order milk.

Lisa does not like meat.

Michael likes juice more than milk.

Chase likes Swiss cheese.

	Plain Cheese	Ham and Cheese	Bacon and Swiss Cheese	Milk	Chocolate Milk	Orange Juice
Lisa						
Michael						
Chase						

Meatball Muncher

Most Meatballs Eaten in One Minute
March 8, 2010

In Japan, Takeru Kobayashi is one of the biggest names in sports. Kobayashi doesn't represent baseball, golf, or swimming though. Instead, he is an International Federation of Competitive Eating (IFOCE) world champion. He is a speed eater. Kobayashi holds world records in both the hot dog and the hamburger categories. In 2010, he added a Guinness World Records record to his menu of awards: the Most Meatballs Eaten in One Minute. Surrounded by fans, this thin young man used a toothpick to eat 29 half-ounce (14 g) cooked meatballs one at a time.

Since he was a teenager, Kobayashi has lived by a personal rule:

"Always be ___ ___ ___ ___ ___ ___ ___ ___ for food."

This rule has served him well in his career as a competitive eater.

● Below are some meatballs. Each meatball contains a letter. The missing word from Kobabyashi's personal rule can be spelled using eight of the letters. Color the meatballs that you think spell the missing word. Hint: The eight colored meatballs will form the shape of the first missing letter. The first letter has been colored for you.

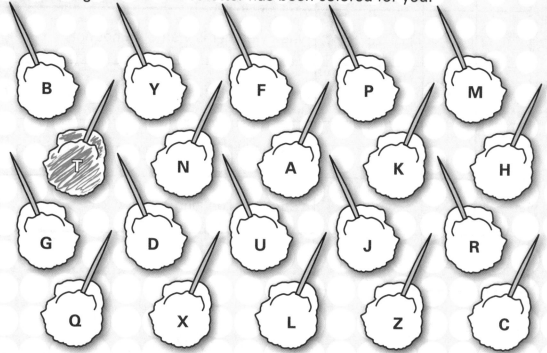

The Boat That Didn't Float

Largest Ice-Cream Boat
April 24, 2004

The Hemglass Sverige AB company in Sweden makes "boats." In fact, the company holds the record for building the largest boat of a particular kind, called a *glassbåt*. Why didn't anyone volunteer to sail off in this huge boat then? The Swedish word *båt* means "boat" in English. But, the Swedish word *glass* means "ice cream." In April 2004, the ice-cream company's employees created a 1,910.3-pound (866.5 kg) ice-cream boat. A smaller version of the glassbåt is a popular item on the company's menu. The

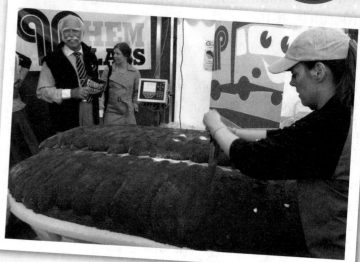

record-setting ice-cream boat was so big that it contained almost as much ice cream, waffle cones, and chocolate topping as 1,200 normal-sized boat treats.

● Ice cream is made from milk and sugar. Ice-cream makers transform these plain ingredients into wonderful ice-cream treats. Starting with the word *milk*, change exactly one letter at a time until you get the word *boat*. Use the clues to help you. The cherry boxes hold the changed letters.

M	I	L	K
				when weather is warm but not hot
				green stuff that sometimes grows on cheese
				what darker type on the computer is called
				a stroke of lightning
B	O	A	T

It's in the Bag!

Largest Bag of Potato Chips
March 11, 2004

Potato chips are great with hamburgers, hot dogs, and sandwiches. They are also great as a snack. But, you would need a lot of friends to help you to finish this record-breaking bag of chips. The Largest Bag of Potato Chips weighed 113 pounds 3 ounces (51.35 kg). That is a lot of potato chips! The Seabrook Potato Crisps Company (UK) made this giant snack bag. Single-serving bags of chips weigh about 1.5 ounces (42.5 g). That means this bag could serve about 1,200 people. It might be a little hard to pass around. And, imagine how much dip you would need!

- There are six bags of potato chips, two each of three brands (Crisps, Dips, and Salty). All of the bags are exactly the same size. One brands' bags weigh more than either of the other two brands' bags. How can you find out which brand of chips has heavier bags by weighing only two bags of chips?

_____

_____

_____

For Big Appetites Only

Largest Steak Commercially Available 1996

The Kestrel Inn in Hatton (UK) is named for one of the smallest birds of prey in the world. But, don't be tricked by the size of the bird. This inn has a reputation for something much larger than a kestrel—its steaks! On the menu is a 12.5-pound (5.7 kg) rump steak. Since first being served in 1996, no one person has ever succeeded in eating the huge piece of meat. Groups of as few as three people have managed to polish it off. However, the closest a single individual has come to eating the entire steak was in 2000 when the owner's son-in-law managed to swallow an amazing 7.5-pound (3.5 kg) steak. That's like eating about 30 hamburger patties!

● Written on the steak below are some letters. The letters that occur in the phrase *FILLING FOOD* have been "eaten." Cross out those letters. The leftover letters, in order, will spell the words that one diner said after her unsuccessful five-hour attempt to eat the entire steak. Write her words on the lines provided.

FOMDYFJLGAGWILS
OILAGNCLLIOHIDEF

" __ __   __ __ __ __ __   __ __ __."

CD-104547

© Carson-Dellosa

A Ton of Cereal

Largest Bowl of Cereal
July 2, 2007

No, this cereal bowl does not belong to a giant. But, it would be large enough for one! The world's Largest Bowl of Cereal measured 8 feet 6 inches (2.6 m) in diameter and stood 4 feet 11 inches (1.5 m) high. That is about the size of a large hot tub. The bowl itself weighed 572 pounds 1 ounce (259.5 kg) and was filled with Kellogg's Corn Flakes. Together, the bowl and the cereal weighed 2,204 pounds 10 ounces (1,000 kg). That really was a ton of cereal. A ton is equal to 2,000 pounds.

● It would take a lot of boxes of cereal to equal the amount used in the Largest Bowl of Cereal. Look at the unfolded boxes below. Circle the box that could be folded to form a cereal box like the one shown.

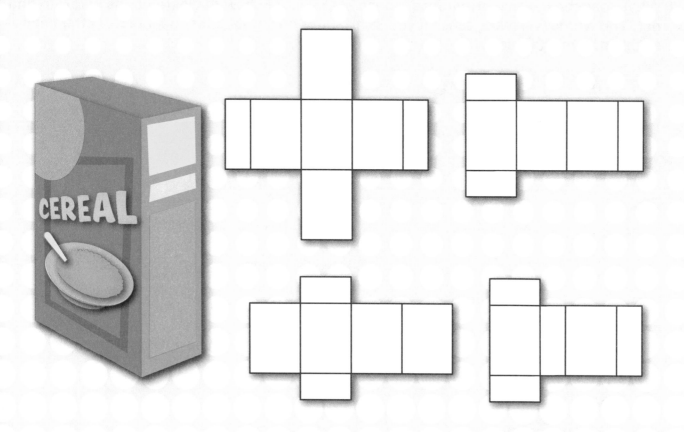

Dessert Rink

Largest Tiramisù
October 30, 2009

What is *tiramisù*? It contains cheese, but it is not a sauce. It contains sugar and chocolate, but it is not candy. It contains eggs and coffee, but it is not breakfast. It even contains cookies, but it is not a snack. So, what is it? Tiramisù is a delicious Italian dessert. It is made up of layers of all of those ingredients. In 2009, Chokogou & L'Essor du Grand Chocolat (France) whipped up an enormous tiramisù for the city of Lyon's Chocolate Fair. To keep the dessert cool, chefs built it on top of an indoor ice rink! By the time the dozens of chefs had finished, the record-breaking dessert took up a 26.25-foot (8 m) by 23.62-foot (7.2 m) section of ice. The tiramisù weighed 2,372 pounds (1,075.92 kg). It wasn't shaped in the usual rectangle or square though. It was built in the shape of a map of France.

● What does the Italian word *tiramisù* mean in English? Follow the instructions below to find out. The words will make sense if you think about how good most people feel after eating such a delicious dessert.

TIRAMISÙ

_____

_____

_____

_____

"___ ___ ___ ___–

___ ___ – ___ ___!"

1. Change the RA to CK.

2. Reverse the last two letters.

3. Change the first and last letters to P.

4. Change the second I to E.

5. Rewrite the new word on the lines.

Mama Tamale

Longest Tamale
May 5, 2006

On a spring day in 2006, chefs at the El Chico Café in Jackson, Tennessee (USA), made a tamale. That may not sound very exciting because El Chico is a Mexican restaurant that always makes tamales. But, this wasn't your everyday tamale. This was a mouthwatering, stomach-growling, finger-licking tamale that was 51 feet 9 inches (15.78 m) long!

The El Chico Café started with Adelaida "Mama" Cuellar's cooking. In 1926, Mama sold her homemade chili and tamales at a local fair. People loved her cooking so much that her sons decided to open a restaurant with Mama as the head cook. Mama's cooking was so good that people even made up stories about her. Some people said she had tomato sauce in her blood. Others said she loved her enchiladas as much as her children, and she had 12!

● Using the word bank, complete the word search. The remaining letters, in order from top to bottom and left to right, will spell another Mama legend.

"How did Mama make guacamole from an avocado?"

She made it ___ ___ ___ ___   ___ ___ ___   ___ ___ ___ ___ ___ ___ ___ ___ ___

___ ___ ___   ___ ___ ___ ___ ___ ___ ___ ___!

c	h	i	m	i	c	h	a	n	g	a	j
t	u	s	t	n	a	c	h	o	u	b	t
o	y	s	e	n	c	h	i	l	a	d	a
r	f	a	j	i	t	a	n	t	c	a	m
t	q	u	e	s	o	l	p	a	a	p	a
i	s	a	l	s	a	u	i	c	m	n	l
l	g	h	e	r	f	p	i	o	o	n	e
l	g	q	u	e	s	a	d	i	l	l	a
a	b	u	r	r	i	t	o	e	e	r	s
c	h	i	l	i	t	o	r	n	a	d	o

Word Bank

burrito	quesadilla
chalupa	queso
chili	salsa
chimichanga	taco
enchilada	tamale
fajita	tornado
guacamole	tortilla
nacho	

CD-104547

A Monster-Sized Matzo Ball

Largest Matzo Ball
June 8, 2009

If at first you don't succeed, try and try again. Noam Sokolow (USA) knows this lesson well. It took him 18 tries to create the world's Largest Matzo Ball. A matzo ball is a ball-shaped dumpling made from matzo meal. Matzo meal is like flour and is ground from unleavened bread, which is like a cracker. To make the record-setting matzo ball, Sokolow started with 200 pounds (91 kg) of matzo meal. Then, he added 1,000 eggs, 80 pounds (36 kg) of margarine, and 20 pounds (9 kg) of chicken base. The resulting matzo ball was 29 inches (74 cm) wide and stood 3 feet (91 cm) tall, which is about the size of a tall trash can. The ball weighed a whopping 267 pounds (121 kg)!

● A local grocery store sells the ingredients for matzo balls in the sizes shown. Complete the shopping list below to show how much of each item you would need to make the record-breaking matzo ball.

Chicken Base
16 ounces

Matzo Meal
12 ounces

Margarine
12 ounces

One Dozen Eggs

Shopping List

_____ dozen eggs

_____ margarine tubs

_____ chicken base containers

_____ matzo meal boxes

What a Classy Dog!

Most Expensive Hot Dog
July 23, 2010

When is a hot dog not a hot dog? When it's an *haute* dog! The Most Expensive Hot Dog in the world is the Foot-Long Haute Dog. *Haute* is a French word meaning *fashionable* or *high-class*. This $69 hot dog is definitely high-class. You can't buy it at the ballpark. It is only served at the Serendipity 3 restaurant in New York City. What makes this hot dog so expensive? First, it is grilled in white truffle oil. A truffle is an extremely expensive kind of mushroom. Then, it is topped off with duck *foie gras*, another French phrase that means *fatty liver*. Even the ketchup and mustard served on the hot dog are of the best quality. When was the last time you saw heirloom tomato ketchup or truffle Dijon mustard at the grocery store?

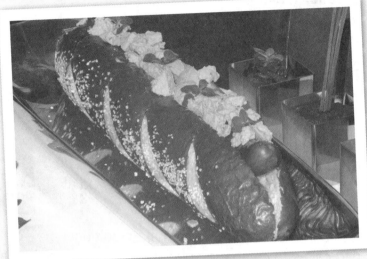

● The Foot-Long Haute Dog still looks like a hot dog, despite its cost. The hot dog bun and the hot dog below are made up of letters. The words *HOT* and *DOG* have been circled for you. How many other three-letter words can you make from the remaining letters? Your words must contain a letter from each section of the hot dog, in any order (top bun, hot dog, bottom bun). Circle the letters as you use them and list your words in the spaces provided. Use each letter only once.

hot		
dog		

D H N T M U S F G J A M I P

F A C E R R T I I B O G L M

H Y A A K O T T T A P E D A

CD-104547

Largest Rice Cake
October 7, 2007

When you think of a rice cake, do you think of the small, crunchy rice treat? This record-breaking rice cake was not small or crunchy. The world's Largest Rice Cake measured 12 feet (3.7 m) in diameter and weighed 8,113 pounds (3.68 tonnes). It was made with steamed rice and was soft and spongy. Kwak Sungho (South Korea) and his team made the colossal cake. It was displayed at the World Rice Food Festival.

In some cultures, people make traditional rice cakes to celebrate special occasions. People make the cakes in different colors for different occasions. White cakes are for good luck. Red cakes are for scaring away bad events, and rainbow-colored cakes are for making dreams come true. This giant cake was for breaking a record!

● Fill in the missing boxes to complete the rice cake puzzle. The column at the right shows the sum of each row. The row at the bottom shows the sum of each column.

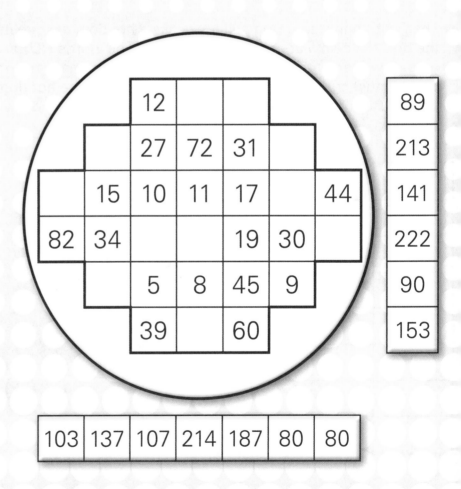

							Row Sum
		12					89
		27	72	31			213
	15	10	11	17		44	141
82	34			19	30		222
		5	8	45	9		90
		39		60			153
103	137	107	214	187	80	80	

He Is Stuffed!

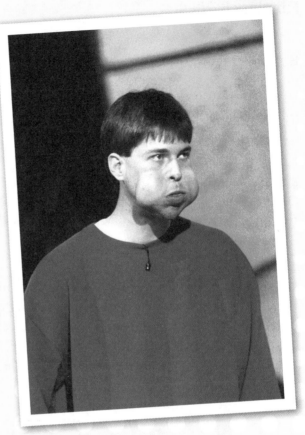

Most Hamburger Stuffing
June 17, 1998

Johnny Reitz (USA) holds the record for the Most Hamburger Stuffing. Reitz wasn't just stuffing toppings onto his burger; he was stuffing burgers into his mouth. And, he wasn't allowed to swallow! Reitz set the record in 1998 when he held three regular burgers, plus buns and toppings, inside his mouth at the same time. How did he manage it? Reitz has his large cheeks to thank. Reitz did not think up this record-breaking eating behavior because he has bad table manners! He tried it out as an act for a talent show he participated in while he was in college.

● Burger patties are usually brown. Burger buns are usually white. But, the toppings you put on your burger can be all different colors. Below is a list of common burger toppings. Using only the letters found in the phrase *hamburger stuffing*, complete the topping words. Use the color words as clues. Hint: These letters can be used more than once.

Toppings		
___ ___ ___ ___ ___ ___ d (yellow)		k ___ ___ c ___ ___ p (red)
___ ___ l ___ ___ ___ (green)		l ___ ___ ___ ___ c ___ (green)
___ o ___ ___ ___ o (red)		o ___ ___ o ___ ___ (white)
c ___ ___ ___ ___ ___ (yellow)		p ___ c k l ___ ___ (green)

Let Them Eat Cake

Largest Wedding Cake
February 8, 2004

The wedding cake is a popular wedding tradition. But, this record holder really takes the cake! It is the world's Largest Wedding Cake. The seven-tiered cake stood 17 feet (5.1 m) tall, and it weighed 15,052 pounds (6.8 tonnes). That's heavier than five small cars! The cake was large enough to feed 59,000 people. Lynn Mansel (USA) and his team of 57 chefs used 700 smaller cakes and two forklifts to create the gigantic cake. The chefs covered the vanilla cake with buttercream and almond frosting. It was displayed at a bridal fair at the Mohegan Sun Hotel in Connecticut.

- The largest wedding cake was made from 700 18-inch by 24-inch cakes. The rectangles below represent 18-inch by 24-inch cakes. Draw lines to show how each cake would be cut to make the pieces equal in size. Then, write the number of servings.

1.

2"x 2" pieces = _____ servings

2.

$1\frac{1}{2}$"x $1\frac{1}{2}$" pieces = _____ servings

3.

$1\frac{1}{2}$"x 2" pieces = _____ servings

4.

2"x 3" pieces = _____ servings

Chocolate-Lovers' Delight

Largest Chocolate Fountain
April 28, 2008

Chocolate lovers will love this sweet record! The Largest Chocolate Fountain stands 26 feet 3 inches (8 m) tall. Six pumps circulate about 4,409 pounds (2 tons) of chocolate through the floor-to-ceiling fountain. The fountain is heated to keep the white, medium, and dark chocolate melted and flowing. The melted chocolate moves at a rate of 120 quarts (114 L) per minute.

It took two years to plan and build the yummy fountain, which is displayed at the Jean Philippe Patisserie (USA) in the Bellagio Hotel in Las Vegas, Nevada. The fountain is kept behind glass. No tasting is allowed!

● Let's talk about chocolate! A box of chocolates has 6 plain milk chocolates, 4 milk chocolates with nuts, 3 milk chocolates with caramel filling, 3 dark chocolates, 3 dark chocolates with nuts, 3 white chocolates, and 2 white chocolates with nuts. Read and answer the questions. Write the letter of each answer on the correct line to help you solve the riddle.

If you choose a piece of candy without looking, what is the probability that it will be milk chocolate?	____ M
If you choose a piece of candy without looking, what is the probability that it will have nuts?	____ E
If you choose a piece of candy without looking, what is the probability that it will be white chocolate?	____ H
If you choose a piece of candy without looking, what is the probability that it will be dark chocolate?	____ O
If you choose a piece of candy without looking, what is the probability that it will have caramel filling?	____ T
If you choose a piece of candy without looking, what is the probability that it will be milk chocolate with nuts?	____ B

What is the worst thing to find in a box of chocolates?

____ ____ ____
1:8   5:24   3:8

____ ____ ____ ____ ____ ____
1:6 1:4 1.8 1:8 1:4 13:24

CD-104547

Onion Energy

Fastest Time to Eat a Raw Onion
August 30, 2009

Do you like chopped green onion in your salad, pan-fried onions with your steak, or breaded onion rings with your burger? That's how most people enjoy eating onions. But, would you eat an entire raw onion? No way!

Believe it or not, some people enjoy chomping down on juicy onions. In 2009, onion-eater Akira Kudo (Japan) attended the Genki Ippai Festa. He set the world record for the Fastest Time to Eat a Raw Onion. Kudo wolfed it down in just 45 seconds! This wasn't just a mini-onion bulb either. The peeled onion had to weigh at least 7.4 ounces (210 g). That's almost half a pound! *Genki Ippai* means "full of energy." Kudo was definitely full of energy that day!

● Onions are made up of layers. If you peel off each layer, you will eventually reach the bulb. Below is an onion containing the phrase *Guinness World Records*. Follow the instructions to peel off the onion layers by crossing out certain letters. Unscramble the remaining letters to spell a word.

GUINNESS

WORLD

RECORDS

1. Peel off the first and the last letter of each word.

2. Peel off all of the E's.

3. Peel off all of the letters that occur in the alphabet after the letter P.

4. Peel off all of the consonants that occur in the alphabet before M.

5. Unscramble the remaining letters.

___ ___ ___ ___ ___

Juice Jumping

Most Juice Extracted from Grapes in One Minute by Stomping
November 9, 2008

Martina Servaty grew up in a small German town famous for its grapes. She studied grapes in college and currently works in the grape industry. In 2008, Servaty made it into the ranks of Guinness World Records record holders. Her record, of course, concerned grapes. In a single minute, Servaty stomped on enough fresh grapes to create 1.19 gallons (5.4 L) of delicious juice. That's about 19 cups of grape juice. Stomping on grapes is a real workout. Some people still harvest juice in this traditional manner, but most farmers extract the juice using automated pressing machines. The machines generate juice at a much faster rate than Servaty's feet and are much less messy!

● To find and solve the riddle below, fill in the clumps of grapes with a matching word from the word bank. The grape clumps contain words the same length as the word bank words. Be careful! Some words have the same number of letters, but only one riddle will make sense.

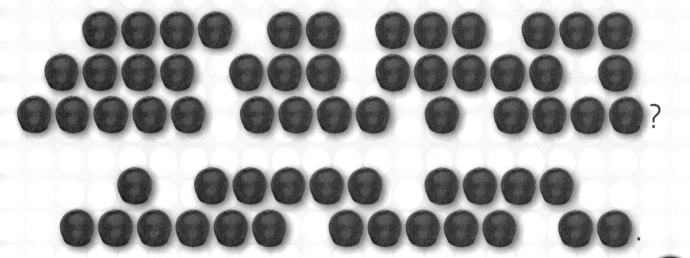

Word Bank

a	cross	grape	nobody	that	with
a	do	grape	on	what	you
a	get	lion	picks	when	you

CD-104547

Salad on the Menu

Largest Salad
June 19, 2010

The Largest Salad in the world was made without a single leaf of lettuce. It was a Greek salad, and the main ingredient was tomato. When K.E.D.I. (The Public Benefit Municipal Enterprise of Ierapetra, Greece) decided to break this record, getting six tons (5.4 tonnes) of ripe tomatoes was essential. But, it wasn't difficult. Ierapetra is a city on the Greek island of Crete. The city is famous for its tomatoes and other fruits and vegetables. It is also famous for its olive oil.

The Largest Salad also contained cucumber, onion, green pepper, and feta cheese. The salad was flavored with olive oil, oregano, and salt. More than 600 volunteers helped with the salad by hauling crates, washing tomatoes, cutting onions, and then putting together the 29,579-pound (13,417 kg) salad. It was worth the effort. Ierapetra received a Guinness World Records record, and fresh Greek salad was distributed to shelters across the island.

The giant salad was one of the big events in Ierapetra's *agrotokosmou* ("rural world") festival celebrating farming. Another big but much messier event was the *ntomatoploemo* ("tomato war"). In this event, locals and visitors alike pelted each other with hundreds of tomatoes until everyone was covered with tomato pulp and seeds. Talk about "seeing red"!

● Using the clues on the following page, fill in the crossword puzzle. Use information from the passage above if you need help.

Across

2. Ierapetra has many greenhouses. A greenhouse is a place where plants _____ inside.

5. A Greek person comes from this country.

6. Ierapetra is the most southern _____ in Europe.

8. In an *ntomatoploemo*, teams throw ripe _____ at each other.

10. Oregano is a type of _____.

12. A green salad usually has a lot of this leafy vegetable.

13. Olives are the fruit of this kind of tree.

14. You probably use _____ and pepper shakers.

Down

1. Is a tomato a fruit or a vegetable?

2. Peppers come in several colors, including this color.

3. What does the *I* probably represent in the initials *K.E.D.I.*?

4. What does an *agrotokosmou* festival celebrate?

6. Feta _____ is made from sheep's or goat's milk.

7. Yes or no: The city of Ierapetra is an island.

8. The Largest Salad used about three times as many tons of tomatoes as cucumbers. About how many tons of cucumbers were used?

9. What do you think the Greek word *salata* means in English?

11. Long, skinny green cucumbers are pickled to make long, skinny dill _____.

A Towering Record

Tallest Sugar Cube Tower
November 12, 2009

Sugar cubes can be used to sweeten a drink or give a horse a sweet treat. However, Paul Van den Nieuwenhof (Belgium) used the cubes to set a record. He built the Tallest Sugar Cube Tower. It measured 6 feet 2 inches (1.9 m) tall. That is taller than most men and women.

To meet the requirements, the tower's base could be no wider than 4 inches (10 cm). A sugar cube measures about one-half inch (1.5 cm) on all sides. It is equal to about a teaspoon of sugar. Van den Nieuwenhof carefully stacked 1,753 sugar cubes to build the record-setting tower. It took him 2 hours, 12 minutes to complete it. Van den Nieuwenhof probably held his breath many times, since the higher the tower grew, the greater the possibility that it might topple. But his patience paid off in a new world record!

- Look at the pattern below. Complete the chart to see how many sugar cubes it would take to make a 10 x 10 x 10 cube.

Cube Size	Number of Sugar Cubes
1 x 1 x 1	1
2 x 2 x 2	8
3 x 3 x 3	27
4 x 4 x 4	
5 x 5 x 5	
6 x 6 x 6	
7 x 7 x 7	
8 x 8 x 8	
9 x 9 x 9	
10 x 10 x 10	

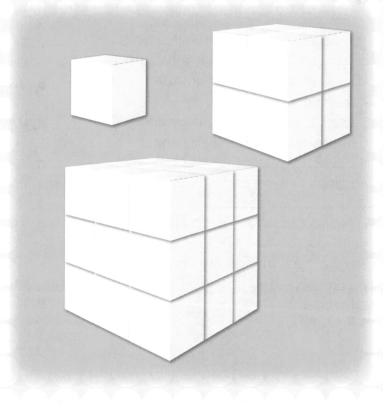

Please Pass the Pasta

Fastest Time to Eat a Bowl of Pasta
November 12, 2009

How do you eat your spaghetti noodles? People eat spaghetti noodles in many different ways. Some eat their noodles using a fork. Some use a spoon to help wind the noodles around the fork. Some use a knife to cut the noodles. And, some just scoop and slurp their noodles. This record setter did just that and ate his noodles fast! The setting for this record was the Ristorante Sant'Eustorgio in Italy. The tables were covered with white tablecloths, and the red-and-white-checkered napkins were neatly folded. Four men sat at the tables, ready to set a record. But, only one man came out the victor. Ernesto Cesario (Italy) ate a bowl of spaghetti noodles in 1 minute, 30 seconds. With his victory, he slurped his way to Guinness World Records fame. This was just one of the many records set in celebration of Guinness World Records Day 2009.

● Use the digits from 0 to 9 to solve the problems and figure out how many pasta noodles are in each bowl.

Problem 1:
```
      □ 3
  ×   2 6
  -------
    2 5 8
    8 □ 0
  -------
  1, 1 1 □
```

Problem 2:
```
      2 9
  ×   5 □
  -------
      2 □
  1 4 □ 0
  -------
  1, 4 □ 9
```

Problem 3:
```
      □ 8
  ×   6 5
  -------
    1 9 □
  2 2 8 0
  -------
  □ , 4 7 0
```

Largest Paella
March 8, 1992

If you ever visit Valencia, Spain, you will have to try *paella* (pronounced *pah-ay-yah*). Paella is a yellowish-orange rice dish. Its color comes from a spice called saffron. *Paella* means "pan." But, you don't eat the pan. You eat what's inside the pan. Different chefs add different types of meat and seafood to the rice.

In Valencia, enormous paellas are often served at festivals and other large gatherings. In 1992, Valencian chef Juan Carlos Galbis and a bunch of helpers cooked the Largest Paella ever made. Galbis used a specially made frying pan that measured 65 feet 7 inches (20 m) across. That's more than 15 feet (4.6 m) wider than a basketball court. The record-setting paella ended up feeding 100,000 people!

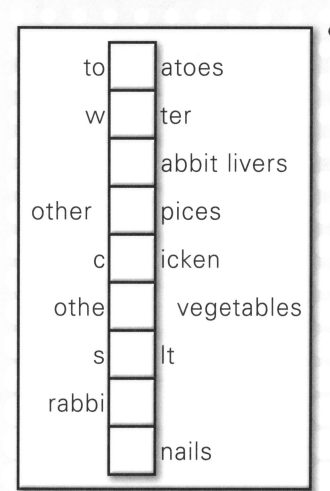

to[ ]atoes
w[ ]ter
[ ]abbit livers
other[ ]pices
c[ ]icken
othe[ ] vegetables
s[ ]lt
rabbi[ ]
[ ]nails

● One of the ingredients that made this enormous paella special was duck. Listed to the left are the other ingredients, each missing one letter. Fill in the missing letters. Those letters, in order from top to bottom, will spell the answer to this question:

In eighteenth-century Valencia, what kind of meat did fishermen add to their paella?

__ __ __ __ __ __ __ __

Anniversary Kiss

Largest Individual Chocolate
July 7, 2007

Chocolate lovers around the world sat up and took notice, especially those who loved Hershey's Kisses. That's because the 100th anniversary chocolate Kiss on display at Chocolate World was not just a piece of chocolate candy. It was a record-breaking 30,540-pound (13,853 kg) Hershey's Kiss! Hershey's Kisses were first made in 1907. The giant anniversary Kiss contained enough milk chocolate to make more than 3 million regular-sized Kisses. It stood 12 feet (3.7 m) tall and measured 10.5 feet (3.2 m) across the bottom.

Hershey's Kisses now come in different flavors. How did Kisses get their name? No one knows for sure. But, the name "Hugs," another Kiss variety, is easier to figure out. Hugs are milk chocolate Kisses surrounded, or "hugged," by a white cream coating.

● We use many words together in pairs similar to Hugs and Kisses. Here are two lists. Every word in List 1 can be paired with one scrambled word in List 2. Unscramble the words in List 2 and write them in the spaces provided. For each of the unscrambled words, find the matching word in List 1. Write the number in the space provided. The first one has been done for you. Be careful! There may be more than one correct answer.

	List 1				List 2
1	hugs		1.	kisses	eiksss
___	black		2.	_____	afilmy
___	boys		3.	_____	berttu
___	bread		4.	_____	ceikoos
___	cats	**and**	5.	_____	cipsy
___	friends		6.	_____	dgos
___	hot		7.	_____	ehitw
___	milk		8.	_____	enosst
___	rock		9.	_____	gilrs
___	sticks		10.	_____	llor
___	twist		11.	_____	nrtu

No Loafing Here!

Largest Loaf of Bread
November 13, 2008

Joaquim Goncalves (Brazil) was not loafing around when he set the record for the Largest Loaf of Bread. It weighed 3,463 pounds (1.5 tonnes)! A lot of work and a ton of flour went into creating this large loaf of bread. Goncalves made the loaf in celebration of Guinness World Records Day. An average loaf of bread weighs about 1 pound 8 ounces (700 g). The record-setting loaf is about the size of 2,308 average-sized loaves of bread. Although this loaf looks long, it does not hold the record for the Longest Loaf of Bread. That loaf of bread is 3,975 feet (1,211.6 m) long. It was made in Portugal in July 2005.

● Solve for each missing variable. To solve the riddle, match the numbers and write the letters on the lines.

$(34 + O) \div 6 = 9$

O = _____

$72 \div (3 + E) = 8$

E = _____

$(L \div 7) \times 5 = 35$

L = _____

$12 + (N \div 5) = 21$

N = _____

$(9 \times 8) \div 2 = H$

H = _____

$T \times (15 + 6) = 504$

T = _____

$(6 \times R) - 15 = 63$

R = _____

Where did the smart loaf of bread end up?

$\overline{}$ $\overline{}$ $\overline{}$ $\overline{}$ $\overline{}$ $\overline{}$ $\overline{}$ $\overline{}$ $\overline{}$ $\overline{}$ $\overline{}$ $\overline{}$ $\overline{}$ $\overline{}$
 20   45   24   36   6   36   20   45   20   13   13   20   49   49

Two Pies Each

Most People in a Pie Fight
November 9, 2008

Pies are made to be eaten, right? Try telling that to the students at the Lawrenceville School (USA) in New Jersey. In 2010, teenagers there set a record for the Most People in a Pie Fight. And, not a single one of the 671 participating students got in trouble! That's because this was an organized food fight. Students and volunteers cooked 1,541 chocolate custard pies for the event. They ended up raising more than $15,000 for charity.

Each participant started the food fight with two pies. Just how much fun was it? "The most fun ever," said a student. He got rid of his pies almost immediately by clapping someone right in the face. Other students raced around the field, trying to find the perfect target. Some even came wearing shower caps, preparing for a chocolate shower. "I love chocolate," one girl said, "but not necessarily in my hair."

● There are many different kinds of pie. Below are the names of eight pies. However, each name contains exactly one spelling mistake. Rewrite the correct names for the pies on the lines provided.

1. Shopfly Pie

___ ___ ___ ___ ___ ___ ___ Pie

2. Mustard Pie

___ ___ ___ ___ ___ ___ ___ Pie

3. Glueberry Pie

___ ___ ___ ___ ___ ___ ___ ___ ___ Pie

4. Tweet Potato Pie

___ ___ ___ ___ ___   ___ ___ ___ ___ ___ Pie

5. Mean Pie

___ ___ ___ ___ Pie

6. Poach Pie

___ ___ ___ ___ ___ Pie

7. Banana Creak Pie

___ ___ ___ ___ ___ ___   ___ ___ ___ ___ Pie

8. Rampberry Pie

___ ___ ___ ___ ___ ___ ___ ___ ___ Pie

King of the Burgers

Most Expensive Hamburger
June 18, 2008

Many fast-food restaurants have special burgers. But, one Burger King restaurant in London, England, has outdone itself by creating the king of the burgers known simply as "The Burger." This hamburger set the record for the Most Expensive Hamburger, selling for $186. It has even been called "The Bling Burger." So, what makes this burger so special? It is made from expensive beef, a slice of top-quality ham, onion straws, and other organic ingredients. The bun is also made with truffles, which are rare, expensive mushrooms.

When first created, this limited-edition burger was only available once a week. Now it can be special ordered. The money from the sale of the burgers goes to a charity that helps children. So, if you are feeling hungry and generous, chew on this record breaker!

● People like their burgers served in different ways. If a restaurant offers hamburgers with or without cheese, pickles, ketchup, and lettuce, how many different ways can a customer order a burger? Write your estimate on the line. Then, list all of the possible ways, using *h* for hamburger, *c* for cheese, *p* for pickles, *k* for ketchup, and *l* for lettuce. Count and write how many possible ways.

Your estimate: _____   Actual possible ways: _____

with no ingredients _____

with 1 ingredient _____

with 2 ingredients _____

with 3 ingredients _____

with 4 ingredients _____

CD-104547

Mounds and Mounds of Meatballs

Largest Serving of Meatballs
May 24, 2009

Perhaps you have heard what happened to the meatball when somebody sneezed. According to the song, it rolled off the table and onto the floor. Then, the meatball rolled out of the door. But, no sneeze could send this many meatballs rolling out the door. The Largest Serving of Meatballs weighed almost 689 pounds (312.5 kg)! The Serres Chamber of Commerce and Industry (Greece) made the record-setting serving of meatballs during an event to promote local food. Participants cooked 882 pounds (400 kg) of buffalo meat and 110 pounds (50 kg) of onions. Then, they added 66 pounds (30 kg) of buffalo milk, 16 pounds (7.3 kg) of bread crumbs, 14 pounds (6.3 kg) of spices, and 3 pounds (1.5 kg) of parsley. It took more than four hours to make the meatballs. But, it took less than one hour to eat them!

● Solve the following meatball problem.

Roberto arranged 10 meatballs on his plate like this:

By moving only 3 meatballs, Roberto's meatballs looked like this:

Which 3 meatballs did Roberto move? Circle them.

Gooey Goodies

Largest Cereal Treat
March 14, 2010

What's gooier than a fresh Rice Krispies Treat? How about a 10,314-pound (4,678 kg) Rice Krispies Treat! In 2010, The Learning Channel (TLC) traveled to La Cañada Flintridge, California, to help volunteers build the world's Largest Cereal Treat. The weekend event was filmed for TLC's show *Mega Bites*. A chef, a food scientist, and an engineer provided expert advice on building the marshmallow-topped dessert. The finished goodie measured 12 feet (3.66 m) long, 8 feet (2.44 m) wide, and 7 feet (2.13 m) high, which is about the size of a large bedroom. Hundreds of volunteers helped with the creation. They took turns combining 6,000 pounds (2,800 kg) of marshmallows with 900 pounds (400 kg) of melted butter and 3,000 pounds (1,400 kg) of crispy rice cereal. Was it worth all of those sticky fingers? Absolutely! The delicious fund-raiser helped raise money to save the children's art program at La Cañada's Community Center.

● Rice Krispies are famous for their Snap, Crackle, and Pop. Hidden in the word search are several sound words. Using the word bank, cross out the words as you find them. The remaining letters, in order from top to bottom and left to right, will spell how many pounds each of the Largest Cereal Treat's crowning giant marshmallows weighed.

C	R	A	C	K	L	E	B	B	T
Z	A	P	R	O	A	R	O	U	H
O	T	H	U	M	P	F	I	Z	Z
O	T	I	N	K	L	E	N	Z	S
M	L	R	C	P	I	N	G	M	Q
U	E	W	H	O	O	S	H	U	U
T	H	U	D	G	R	O	A	N	I
T	I	E	B	L	E	A	T	C	S
E	S	W	O	O	S	H	E	H	H
R	S	N	A	P	P	L	U	N	K

Word Bank

bleat	munch	swoosh
boing	mutter	thud
buzz	ping	thump
crackle	plunk	tinkle
crunch	rattle	whoosh
fizz	roar	zap
groan	snap	zoom
hiss	squish	

_____ _____ _____ _____ _____

Largest Ice Pop
August, 1997

One of the most popular ice pops in the world is the "Rocket." It got its name from its rocket shape. A Dutch ice-cream company, Iglo-Ola, first created this frozen treat in 1962. At that time, rockets were on everyone's mind. People had first rocketed into space just the year before. In 1997, Jan van den Berg (Netherlands) decided to celebrate a Dutch holiday by making an enormous Rocket ice pop. He was able to use Iglo-Ola's Rocket expertise. Tons of water and sugar later, van den Berg's Rocket ice pop stood 21.3 feet (6.5 m) tall. If it had melted, the remarkable ice pop could have made 250,000 ice cubes! Its official weight was 20,020 pounds (9.081 tonnes). But best of all, it still contained the Rocket's three traditional flavors: pineapple on the bottom, orange in the middle, and raspberry on the top.

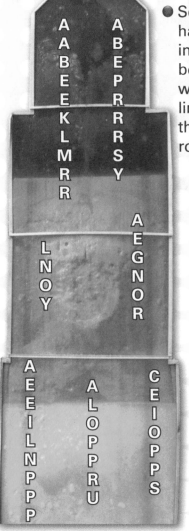

● Seven words from the passage have been scrambled and frozen in this Rocket ice pop. The bottom words start with *p*. The middle words start with *o*. The top words start with *r*. Unscramble the words and write them on the lines provided. The circled letters, in numbered order, will spell the name of the first manned American rocket in space. Hint: This rocket was named after the planet closest to the sun.

1. r _ ◯ _ _ _ _ _ _

2. p _ _ ◯ _ _ _ _

3. o ◯ _ _ _ _

4. i ◯ _ _ _ _ _ _

5. p _ _ ◯ _ _ _

6. r _ _ _ _ _ ◯ _ _

7. o _ _ ◯ _

_ _ _ _ _ _ _ 3

Caution! Pizza Crossing

Most Pizza Rolls Across the Shoulder in 30 Seconds
April 20, 2006

Tony Gemignani (USA) is a pizza master! He has earned many pizza titles and awards. He even owns a pizza school. Gemignani has also set the record for the Most Pizza Rolls Across the Shoulders in 30 Seconds. Being able to roll 20 ounces (567 g) of pizza dough across the shoulders is impressive. But, being able to roll the dough across the shoulders 37 times in 30 seconds is amazing! Gemignani set the record during the filming of the Food Network's Guinness World Records week in Minneapolis, Minnesota.

● Each of the following pizzas has been divided into 16 smaller pieces. Pieces have been eaten from each pizza. Which two pizzas, if placed on top of each other, will form a whole pizza?

It's Delish!

Largest Serving of Fried Chicken
May 30, 2009

The delicious taste of Kentucky Fried Chicken (KFC) has been around since 1940. That's when Colonel Sanders came up with the recipe. Now, KFC restaurants are all over the world. Every one of them sells buckets of the colonel's crispy chicken. The colonel would have been surprised at how many pieces were tucked into a bucket on May 30, 2009, in Kuwait. Employees at the Kuwait Food Company Americana managed to fit 5,400 pieces into a nearly 5-foot-tall (1.5 m) bucket. Weighing 1,279 pounds (580 kg), a single person couldn't have carried that bucket home for dinner! Luckily, all of the food was donated to charity. It's a long way from the state of Kentucky to the Middle Eastern country of Kuwait. It's 6,870 miles (11,056 km) to be exact. But, a Kentucky KFC piece of chicken is pretty similar to a Kuwait KFC piece. It's just a strange coincidence that it was the **K**uwait **F**ood **C**ompany that brought the **k**itchen-**f**resh **c**hicken of **K**entucky **F**ried **C**hicken to Kuwait.

● The bucket below contains 6 sets of 3 pieces of chicken, for a total of 18 pieces of chicken. Each chicken piece contains a word starting with K, F, or C. Using the words, put together 6 platefuls of chicken. Each plate should contain exactly one K, F, and C piece. The K, F, and C words on each plate should belong together in some way.

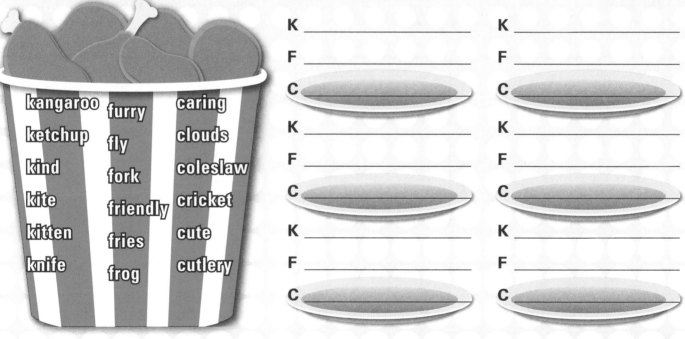

kangaroo   furry   caring
ketchup   fly   clouds
kind   fork   coleslaw
kite   friendly   cricket
kitten   fries   cute
knife   frog   cutlery

K _____   K _____
F _____   F _____
C _____   C _____

K _____   K _____
F _____   F _____
C _____   C _____

K _____   K _____
F _____   F _____
C _____   C _____

CD-104547

One Potato, Two Potato

Largest Serving of French Fries
February 19, 2004

Would you like fries with that? That is a common question asked when ordering a burger or a sandwich at a fast-food restaurant. A large serving of french fries weighs about 7 ounces (198 g). The record-breaking Largest Serving of French Fries weighed 812 pounds (368.5 kg)! Alan Williams (UK) at Hereford Racecourse made this generous serving. He used more than 60 bags of potatoes. Can you imagine cutting up that many potatoes? Williams and his crew used a line of large fryers to cook the potatoes. Next, the crew placed the fries in a bag that was 3 feet by 3 feet (1 m). The money raised from the sale of the fries was donated to charity.

FRENCH FRIES

Large (9 oz.) $2.00

Medium (6 oz.) .. $1.50

Small (4 oz.) $1.00

● Rusty's dad gave him $5.00 to buy fries for Rusty and his three brothers. Show three different ways that Rusty can spend the money on the fries. Then, circle the way that Rusty and his brothers will get the most fries for $5.00.

The Wall Against Hunger

Largest Canned Food Structure
August 25, 2010

The Vietnam Veterans Memorial in Washington, D.C., is composed of polished black granite. This memorial wall measures 247 feet (75.3 m) long. It was built to honor soldiers from the Vietnam War. In 2010, volunteers at North Hardin HOPE (USA) built a smaller replica of this famous memorial in Elizabethtown, Kentucky. Their wall measured 162.68 feet (49.6 m) long and 5.01 feet (1.5 m) high. But, instead of being made of stone, it was made up of 134,722 carefully stacked cans of food. North Hardin HOPE named their wall "The Wall Against Hunger." The group's goal wasn't just to set a world record. It also wanted to collect donations for local food pantries. Both goals were achieved.

● The word *HOPE* is an acronym that represents the first letters of the words *Helping Other People Everyday. HOPE* can also be created from the first letters of labeled cans of Ham, Onions, Pears, and Eggplant. Below are several stacks of canned foods. Read the food labels on the cans. For each stack of cans, unscramble the first letters of each label to discover the associated word. Write your answers on the lines provided. Hint: The unscrambled words appear somewhere in the above passage.

_____ _____ _____ _____

_____ _____

Fans Flipping Flapjacks

Most People Tossing Pancakes
October 24, 2008

On Friday, 445 fans flipped flapjacks in frying pans. Try saying that three times fast! No, this is not just a silly tongue twister. This is the record for the Most People Tossing Pancakes. Bram Zwiers (Netherlands) set the record on the TV show *Mooi! Weer de Leeuw*. The show was part of the Guinness World Records Day celebration. Each person in the studio audience was given a frying pan and a pancake. On the signal, all 445 people flipped 445 pancakes at the same time and set a new world record.

● Rick made 16 pancakes: 4 plain (P), 4 blueberry (B), 4 chocolate chip (C), and 4 strawberry (S). He placed some of the pancakes on a serving tray as shown below. Write the letters for the remainder of the pancakes on the tray so that 4 of the same types of pancake are not in the same row, column, or long diagonal.

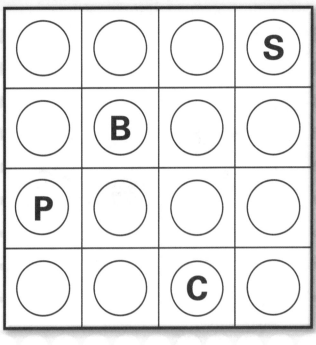

Big Mac, Please

Most Big Macs Consumed
August 17, 2008

For almost 40 years, D. Gorske (USA) has eaten one McDonald's Big Mac nearly every day. He started in 1972. Gorske was so thrilled with his first burger that he made three separate trips to the McDonald's that day, eating a total of nine Big Macs. By 2008, Gorske had swallowed 23,000 "two all-beef patties, special sauce, lettuce, cheese, pickles, onions on a sesame-seed bun." He has even written a book about his obsession. Gorske has eaten a Big Mac in every one of the 50 states, every Major League Baseball park, every National Football League stadium, and every NASCAR track.

How has this McDonald's fan stayed so slim? He walked about 10 miles to and from work every day for years. Have you ever heard the saying "You are what you eat"? D. Gorske doesn't look like a McDonald's Big Mac. But, he is pretty big, standing taller than 6 feet (1.8 m). And, what does the *D* in his name stand for? You guessed it—Donald, of course.

1.

2.

3.

● The Big Macs to the left contain letters on the patties and the buns. Using the clues, write the correct letters to discover what Gorske's former job was.

1. top bun   _____

2. middle bun   _____

3. top patty   _____

4. bottom bun   _____

5. bottom patty   _____

6. top patty   _____

4.

5.

6.

__ __ __ __ __

__ __ __ __

CD-104547

Try Catching This Ball!

Largest Popcorn Ball
September 29, 2006

In the United States, October is National Popcorn Popping Month. In the state of Illinois, popcorn is the official state snack food. So, it was no surprise when employees at The Popcorn Factory in Lake Forest, Illinois, decided to celebrate October 2006 by creating the world's Largest Popcorn Ball. It took two days and tons of popcorn, but they did it. The huge edible ball weighed a whopping 3,423 pounds (1,553 kg). It measured 8 feet (2.4 m) in diameter and had a circumference of 24.5 feet (7.5 m). Compared to a regular popcorn ball, this one was almost 50,000 times larger!

Most people know that popcorn tastes good and is a low-calorie snack. But, did you know that not all corn pops? Of the six types of corn, only one kind pops. It's called popcorn! Popcorn comes in two basic shapes, snowflake and mushroom. It is the number-one food popped in microwaves. It can pop up to three feet in the air. And, here is one more fun fact about popcorn: If you laid a trail of popcorn from the East Coast to the West Coast, from New York City to Los Angeles, you would need more than 300 million popcorn kernels!

● What else do you know about popcorn? For each of the statements on the next page, decide which answer is true. Write the corresponding answer letter in the Popcorn Table. If you are right, the letters, from top to bottom, will spell the answer to this joke:

What do you get when you cross popcorn with ice cream?

" __ __ __ __ __ __ __ __ __ __ "

1. Popcorn

   (A) only comes from a special type of corn.

   (M) can be made from all types of corn.

2. Popcorn

   (Y) always pops into the same type of shape.

   (P) pops into mushroom or snowflake shapes.

3. Popcorn flavors

   (K) are always salty.

   (O) are usually salty or sweet.

4. Popcorn pops because of

   (P) water inside the popcorn kernel.

   (O) air inside the popcorn kernel.

5. Popcorn is usually eaten with

   (O) a spoon.

   (S) your hands.

6. Edible popcorn balls are usually made with

   (I) sticky syrup or sugar.

   (L) glue.

7. Popcorn kernels can pop as high as

   (A) 30 feet (9.1 m).

   (C) 3 feet (0.91 m).

8. Another word for *corn* is

   (I) rice.

   (L) maize.

9. Many people cook popcorn in the

   (E) microwave.

   (D) vacuum cleaner.

Popcorn Table	
Question	Answer Letter
1	
2	
3	
4	
5	
6	
7	
8	
9	

Soup's On!

Largest Bowl of Soup
May 16, 2009

All you need are some crackers and a spoon to enjoy this delicious food record. It is the world's Largest Bowl of Soup. To set this record, workers from DENK Communicatie (Netherlands) prepared 7,042 gallons (26,658 L) of vegetable soup. The cooks started the soup with 4,623 gallons (17,500 L) of water. Then, they added 16,402 pounds (7,440 kg) of tomatoes, 2,755 pounds (1,250 kg) of cucumbers, and 992 pounds (450 kg) of bell peppers. Next, the cooks mixed in some olive oil and tomato paste. To spice it up, the chefs added parsley, garlic, salt, pepper, and basil. Soup's on!

● A fourth-grade class made a large pot of vegetable soup. The soup included tomatoes, onions, bell peppers, carrots, and celery. To complete the recipe, use the clues below to figure out how much of each vegetable was used in the soup.

Vegetable Soup

_____ cups tomatoes

_____ cups carrots

_____ cups onions

_____ cups bell peppers

_____ cups celery

Cut up the vegetables. Add to 6 cups of water.

Simmer until vegetables are soft.

All of the vegetables were cut into bite-sized chunks and measured in standard measuring cups.

Twice as many cups of tomatoes were used than carrots.

Twice as many cups of carrots were used than onions.

One cup each of two vegetables was added to the pot.

$1\frac{1}{2}$ cups of onions were added to the pot.

How Many Pieces Do You Wish?

Largest Bubble Gum Mosaic
August 17, 2004

Bubble gum, bubble gum, in a dish. How many pieces do you wish? This mosaic wished for 100,000 pieces! It set the record for the Largest Bubble Gum Mosaic. A mosaic is a picture made up of small colorful pieces. In this case, the small colorful pieces were wrapped pieces of bubble gum. Several companies got together to set the record: TBWA Digerati, ID Productions, SABC 1, and Cadbury's Chappies (all South Africa). It took five days to complete the mosaic. It measured 209 square feet (19.4 m²). That is about the size of a large pool table.

The completed mosaic revealed a picture of Nelson Mandela. Mandela is known for his dedication to freedom and equality. He led South Africa during a time when the country was experiencing a lot of racial tension. He received the Nobel Peace Prize in 1993 for his efforts to bring peace to South Africa.

● Make the bubble gum in this bubble gum machine more appealing by adding color. Using the clues, color the numbers. Color the numbers using the rules of divisibility.

1. Color the numbers divisible by 2 yellow.

2. Color the numbers divisible by 3 red.

3. Color the numbers divisible by 5 blue.

4. Color the prime numbers green.

CD-104547

Egg-stravaganza

Largest Scrambled Eggs
December 1, 2009

How many eggs do you think go into a plate of scrambled eggs? If you are having a regular breakfast, you are probably thinking two eggs. If you have a big day ahead, you may even be thinking three eggs. But, would you ever think more than 20,000 eggs? That's how many eggs were scrambled at a New Zealand McDonald's on December 1, 2009. Workers used rakes to mix the eggs and the cream in a huge cooking dish. Then, they used shovels to serve the 2,733 pounds 11 ounces (1,240 kg) of eggs, which were

given away for free. Besides setting a record for the Largest Scrambled Eggs, McDonald's promoted its use of free-range eggs from that area of New Zealand. Are free-range eggs different from regular eggs? No, they are not. But, the chickens are different. Free-range chickens wander around the farmyard during the day. Factory-farmed chickens are kept inside all of the time.

● The free-range nest below contains the three unique letters (*e*, *g*, and *n*) that are in the phrase *free-range* but are not in the phrase *factory-farm*. The factory-farm nest contains the five unique letters (*c*, *m*, *o*, *t*, and *y*) that are in *factory-farm* but are not in *free-range*. On the lines provided, write as many words as you can using only these nest letters. You may use each letter as often as you want, even in the same word. For each word, write the number of letters used from each nest.

FREE-RANGE

FACTORY-FARM

F-R	Your Word	F-F	F-R	Your Word	F-F
1	*not*	2			

Largest Muffin
February 27, 2010

Oh, do you know the muffin man? In this case, the muffin man's name is Gerhard Hinz (Germany). He baked the world's Largest Muffin. It weighed 195.5 pounds (88.7 kg)! It was 2 feet 7 inches (79 cm) in diameter, and it stood 1 foot 6 inches (45.5 cm) high. Hinz used more than 110 pounds (50 kg) of wheat flour, 42 pounds (19 kg) of butter, and 176 pounds (5 kg) of marshmallows to make the giant muffin.

As with all big projects, this baker had some help. The pop band Queensberry lent a hand. They helped stir the batter. The popularity of the band also helped promote the event. After the official measurement was taken, organizers gave the muffin away for a donation. The money earned went to help a hospice charity in Germany.

● Find the equivalent decimal for each fraction. To solve the riddle, match the numbers and write the letters on the lines.

$\frac{1}{4}$ = _____ A $\frac{4}{8}$ = _____ E $\frac{3}{10}$ = _____ W $\frac{2}{5}$ = _____ I $\frac{11}{10}$ = _____ N

$\frac{1}{5}$ = _____ R $\frac{4}{5}$ = _____ U $\frac{9}{20}$ = _____ T $\frac{3}{4}$ = _____ M $\frac{3}{20}$ = _____ S

$\frac{3}{5}$ = _____ Y $\frac{1}{10}$ = _____ C $\frac{7}{20}$ = _____ F $\frac{32}{100}$ = _____ L $\frac{4}{25}$ = _____ G

Why did the muffin visit the doctor?

_____ _____   _____ _____ _____
.4   .45   .3   .25   .15

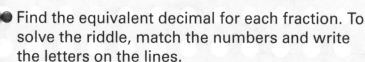

_____ _____ _____ _____ _____ _____ _____   _____ _____ _____ _____ _____ _____!
.35   .5   .5   .32   .4   1.1   .16   .1   .2   .8   .75   .75   .6

A Refreshing Record

Largest Jug of Soft Drink
June 8, 2008

Almost nothing can be more refreshing than a nice cool drink on a hot summer's day. On this summer's day, Kraft Foods (Brazil) created a record-breaking drink that could quench the thirst of a crowd! The drink set the record for the Largest Jug of Soft Drink. The jug was 11 feet 11 inches (3.38 m) tall. Its circumference was 25 feet 9 inches (7.87 m). Participants filled the jug with 2,045 gallons (9,300 L) of water and 4,650 packets of Fresh powder drink. Each packet contained about 2 teaspoons of the powder. Next time you make a pitcher of your favorite drink, remember this enormous jug!

● Imagine that you have a 3-gallon jug and a 5-gallon jug. You need to measure *exactly* 7 gallons of soft drink. How can you do it?

_____

_____

_____

_____

_____

Curry for a Cause

Largest Curry
July 16, 2005

In 2000, chef Abdul Salam (UK) set a record for making the world's Largest Curry. It weighed about 6,000 pounds (3 tonnes). "I was pleased with my three-tonne curry," the Eastern Eye Restaurant owner said. In 2005, Salam tried again. "I want this record to stand for tens, if not hundreds of years," he explained. He and his assistants cooked a massive vegetarian tikka masala curry weighing 22,707.61 pounds (10.3 tonnes)! Salam had planned to make chicken curry. He decided on a vegetarian curry instead. It included a lot of vegetables, water, oil, and spices. A local festival was going on that weekend, so all of that curry didn't go to waste. And, the money raised helped children in Salam's native country of Bangladesh.

● Using the clues, fill in the words below. The answers can be found in the passage above. Each answer begins or ends with a boxed letter. The boxed letters, from top to bottom, will spell the name of a special November day in the United Kingdom.

___ ___ ___ ___ ___ ___ ___ ___ ___ ___ ___ ___ ___ ___ ___ ___ ___

Part of a restaurant name: ___ ___ ___ ___ ___ [ ]

Part of a curry dish name: ___ ___ ___ ___ ___ [ ]

[ ]___ ___ ___ : Part of a curry dish name

". . . [ ]___ not hundreds of years,"

[ ]___ ___ : Ingredient in curry

Ingredient not in this curry: ___ ___ ___ ___ ___ [ ]

[ ]___ ___ [ ] : Salam's first name

[ ]___ ___ ___ : Salam's job title

[ ]___ : Country where Salam lives

Liquid in curry: ___ ___ ___ ___ [ ]

[ ]___ ___ ___ ___ : Something Salam set

What Salam made: ___ ___ ___ ___ [ ]

Something Salam broke: ___ ___ ___ ___ ___ [ ]

[ ]___ ___ ___ : "Word that means "one more time"

What was donated to help children: ___ ___ ___ ___ [ ]

Big Boil and Bake

Largest Bagel
August 27, 2004

A plain mini-bagel makes a great snack. A regular bagel with cream cheese makes a great lunch. What does a giant bagel make? It makes a Guinness World Records record! In 2004, Brueggers Bagels (USA) created an 868-pound (393.7 kg) bagel for the New York State Fair. Brueggers cooked it just like a regular bagel, but for a much longer period of time. Nine cooks worked through the night to first boil (for a half hour) and then bake (for 10 hours) their masterpiece. The result was a crispy-on-the-outside, chewy-on-the-inside bagel measuring 20 inches (51 cm) thick and 6 feet (1.8 m) wide. A special crane had to be used to lift it to the fairgrounds. Did all of this deliciousness go to waste? No, it did not! Fairgoers who made a donation to the food bank were able to taste a slice of the very tasty snack. The only thing missing was about 500 pounds (227 kg) of cream cheese.

● Bagel dough is made up of five simple ingredients: flour, water, yeast, malt, and salt. Below are five bagels. The phrase on each bagel contains the name of an ingredient. Write the correct ingredient names on the lines provided.

_ _ _ _ _ _ _ _   _ _ _ _ _ _ _ _   _ _ _ _ _ _ _ _

_ _ _ _ _ _ _ _   _ _ _ _ _ _ _ _

Cupcake or "Tubcake"?

Largest Cupcake
October 3, 2009

By definition, a cupcake is a cake the size of a cup. But, the world's Largest Cupcake was about the size of a hot tub! It probably should have been called a "tubcake"! It weighed 1,315 pounds (596.47 kg). The cake batter included 340 pounds (154.22 kg) of sugar, 346 pounds (156.94 kg) of eggs, 680 pounds (308.44 kg) of flour, and more. The icing was made with 75 pounds (34 kg) of butter, 75 pounds (34 kg) of shortening, and 200 pounds (90.7 kg) of powdered sugar.

Bakers created the huge cupcake for the Think Pink Rocks concert. Can you guess what color the cupcake was? Pink, of course! It was pale pink with a dark pink cherry on top. The concert raised money for breast cancer research. Global TV Concepts (USA) held the event.

● Write the integers inside each set of three intersecting circles so that the three integers in each circle add up to 0. The first one has been done for you.

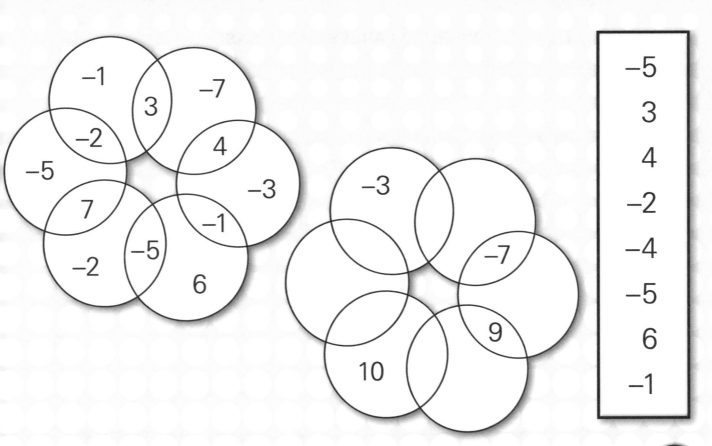

-5
3
4
-2
-4
-5
6
-1

CD-104547

Pizza Acrobat

Largest Pizza Base Spun in Two Minutes
April 20, 2006

If a pizza king is ever named, Tony Gemignani (USA) will probably wear the crown. Gemignani has won dozens of pizza awards, including World Pizza Champion, World Champion Pizza Maker, and Food Network Gold Medalist. He is also a two-time Guinness World Records record holder. The Largest Pizza Base Spun in Two Minutes record shows why Gemignani is also a world champion pizza acrobat. The largest base competition tests how well someone handles pizza dough. To set the record, Gemignani's pizza base measured 33.2 inches (84.33 cm) across. It had smooth, rounded edges and no holes in the dough. World champion pizza-tosser Gemignani passed the test with flying, or was that "tossing," colors!

● Rearrange any or all of the letters in the phrase *WORLD'S LARGEST PIZZA BASE* to make new words. How "large" a word can you create? Without using any of the words in the phrase, such as *base* or *large*, write pairs of your own words on the lines below.

WORLD'S LARGEST PIZZA BASE

____ one-letter words ____

____ ____ two-letter words ____ ____

____ ____ ____ three-letter words ____ ____ ____

____ ____ ____ four-letter words ____ ____ ____

____ ____ ____ ____ five-letter words ____ ____ ____ ____

____ ____ ____ ____ six-letter words ____ ____ ____ ____

____ ____ ____ ____ ____ seven-letter words ____ ____ ____ ____ ____

____ ____ ____ ____ ____ eight-letter words ____ ____ ____ ____ ____

_____ larger words _____

CD-104547

Sweet Jar of Jelly Beans

Largest Jar of Jelly Beans
October 15, 1999

This is a sweet record in more ways than one! This record is for the Largest Jar of Jelly Beans. The jar was 4 feet 6 inches (1.3 m) wide by 4 feet 6 inches (1.3 m) deep and 10 feet (3 m) high. It was filled with 2,160,000 jelly beans, and it weighed 6,050 pounds (2,744.23 kg)! Monica Kasley (USA) from the Empress Hotel in Hammond, Indiana, organized the record-setting event. As a child, Kasley dreamed of setting a Guinness World Records record. She was happy to be a part of this big event and make her dream come true. Jelly Belly Candy Company, who donated the jelly beans, makes jelly beans in 50 flavors and colors. Fortunately, the jelly beans they donated were in one-ounce packages. The small packages made it easy to give away the jelly beans once the record had been broken.

- A fifth-grade class filled a jar with 1,000 jelly beans. The jelly beans were red, yellow, orange, green, black, blue, and purple. Use the clues to figure out how many of each color of jelly bean was in the jar.

Three-tenths of the jelly beans are red.

There are 1/3 fewer purple jelly beans than yellow jelly beans.

There are 1/2 as many yellow jelly beans as red jelly beans.

There is the same number of blue and purple jelly beans.

There are 15 times more red jelly beans than black jelly beans.

There are 30 more green jelly beans than yellow jelly beans.

_____ red   _____ black

_____ yellow   _____ blue   _____ orange

_____ purple   _____ green

Stacker Packer Power

Tallest Cookie Tower
February 29, 2008

Spring is the time for Girl Scouts of the USA troops to sell cookies. To kick off their cookie sale in 2008, Girl Scouts from Mt. Wilson Vista (California) Council (USA) tried something different. With the help of experts, 70 "Stacker Packer Cookie Girls" created the Tallest Cookie Tower in the world. The official height was 5 feet 4 inches (1.62 m), but the girls actually continued adding another 3 inches (7.6 cm) to their masterpiece. It took 16 hours and nearly 20,000 cookies to complete. They created a nine-tiered, 145-layer tower that required the girls to work together as a team.

● Girl Scouts sell many different varieties of cookies. Decode the Girl Scout Cookie names below. The first one has been done for you. Then, follow the alphabet pattern to decode the other cookie names. The circled letters, in order, will spell the names of the two types of cookies used to create the record-breaking tower.

____ ____ ____ ____   ____ ____ ____ ____ ____   and   ____ ____ ____ – ____ ____ ____ – ____ ____ ____

Coded Cookie	Real Cookie
SHDQXW EXWWHU VDQGZLFK	P E A N U (T) B U T T E R S A N D W I C (H)
FDUDPHO GHOLWHV	____ ____ ____ ____ ____ ____ (O) ____ ____ ____ ____ ____ (O) ____ ____ ____
WKDQN X EHUUB PXQFK	(O)____ ____ (O) ____ ____ ____ ____ ____ ____ ____ ____
SHDQXW EXWWHU SDWWLHV	____ ____ ____ ____ ____ ____ ____ ____ ____ ____ ____ ____ ____ ____ ____ (O) ____ ____ ____
OHPRQ FKDOHW FUHPHV	____ ____ ____ ____ (O) ____ ____ ____ ____ ____ ____ ____ ____ ____ (O) ____ ____ ____ ____ ____
WDJDORQJV	____ ____ ____ ____ ____ ____ ____ (O) ____
GXOFH GH OHFKH	____ ____ ____ ____ (O) ____ ____ ____ ____ ____ ____ ____
OHPRQDGHV	____ ____ ____ (O) ____ ____ ____ (O) ____
WUHIRLOV	____ ____ ____ ____ (O) ____ ____ ____
VKRUWEUHDG	____ ____ ____ ____ ____ ____ ____ ____ (O) ____
VKRXW RXWV	____ (O) ____ ____ ____ ____ ____ ____ ____!
WKDQNV-D-ORW	____ ____ ____ ____ ____ (O)-____-____ ____ ____

Say Cheesecake!

Largest Cheesecake
January 25, 2009

Many people think cheesecake is delicious. Many people also think that even if they wanted to, it would be hard to eat a lot of cheesecake at one time. It's just too filling. That's why the organizers behind Philadelphia Kraft Foods Mexico's giant cheesecake creation chose to donate most of their cheesecake instead of eat it. The 4,703-pound (2,134 kg) record-breaking cake measured 8 feet 2 inches (2.5 m) across and 20 inches (56 cm) high. The chefs sliced the cheesecake into more than 20,000 delicious pieces!

● Chefs spent 60 hours creating the cheesecake. They used the following ingredients:

Butter

Cream cheese

Pastry

Strawberries

Sugar

Yogurt

These six ingredients are mixed into this cheesecake. Cross out the ingredients letter by letter as you find them. The leftover letters, unscrambled, will spell the number of chefs who created this dessert.

___ ___ ___ ___ ___ - ___ ___ ___ ___ ___

abcefghimoprstuvwyabcefgirs tuyaaefirstuyaerstersterrer

A Record to Float Your Boat!

Largest Soft Drink Float
May 25, 2007

The saying "whatever floats your boat" means "whatever makes you happy." The float in this record made a lot of people happy. It was the world's Largest Soft Drink Float. It contained 3,000 gallons (13,638 L) of Vanilla Coke and ice cream. Coca-Cola made the float at the World of Coca-Cola Museum in Atlanta, Georgia (USA). Floats come in many different sizes and flavors. The record-setting float was in a glass that was 15 feet (4.57 m) tall. That is about as tall as a single-story house. It had 2,850 gallons (7.57 L) of Vanilla Coke and 7,200 scoops of ice cream. What type of float floats your boat?

● Four friends went to the soda shop. They all ordered different floats. Read the clues and mark the chart to figure out who ordered which type of float.

The girl who ordered the cherry cola had it with cherry vanilla ice cream.

Jessica is allergic to strawberry, but she loves root beer.

Neither of the boys had plain vanilla ice cream.

The boy who ordered cola had it with chocolate ice cream.

Greg loves strawberry ice cream.

	Cola	Root Beer	Lemon-Lime	Cherry Cola	Vanilla	Chocolate	Strawberry	Cherry Vanilla
Deanna								
Greg								
Julio								
Jessica								

Jumbo Shrimp?

Largest Shrimp Cocktail
July 10, 2009

An *oxymoron* is a figure of speech that combines two opposites, such as *pretty ugly* and *jumbo shrimp*. This last oxymoron was used in the making of the world's Largest Shrimp Cocktail, which weighed 219 pounds 13 ounces (99.72 kg). Tom Pickerell of the Seafood Association of Great Britain (UK) created the giant appetizer.

The glass serving dish measured 4 feet 11 inches (1.5 m) high. Pickerell and his assisting chefs placed about 100 pounds (45 kg) of shrimp on top of the 22 pounds (10 kg) of lettuce in the dish. Then, they poured dressing over the shrimp and the lettuce. The dressing included 60 pounds (27.3 kg) of mayonnaise and 32 pounds (14.45 kg) of ketchup. Next, the chefs served the shrimp cocktail to the awaiting crowd. The crowd agreed that the record-setting dish was *awfully good*!

● **Below are 8 shrimp cocktail dishes. Use the clues to figure out how many shrimp are in each dish.**

There are a total of 112 shrimp.

The dish with the fewest shrimp has only 10 shrimp.

Only two dishes have the same number of shrimp.

Only two dishes have an odd number of shrimp.

The dish with the most shrimp has 8 more shrimp than the dish with the fewest shrimp.

None of the dishes has exactly 11 or 17 shrimp.

CD-104547

Largest Tea Party
February 24, 2008

Can you really have fun at a tea party? If you ask the 32,681 people who took part in the Largest Tea Party in the world, the answer would probably be a resounding yes! In 2008, the Indian newspaper company Dainik Bhaskar organized the tea party to celebrate its 25th year of publishing newspapers in the city of Indore. The tea party also raised money to help develop the city. Nearly 1,000 people were needed to serve tea to the thousands of tea drinkers who showed up at the stadium. And, everyone's cup was filled in just 20 minutes! Was a drink of Brooke Bond Red Label tea the only attraction that day? Of course it wasn't! Partygoers were treated to live music and fireworks as well. They were even able to take home their teacups as souvenirs.

● Below are 10 teacups and 10 saucers. The partial word on each teacup fits between two of the letters in the partial word on exactly one saucer to form a real word. These 10 words appear somewhere in the above passage. Match each cup to the appropriate saucer by writing the correct full word on the lines provided below the matching saucer.

Teacups: arg ate bli ery gani ink mpa op trac wsp

Saucers:

cony

tred

neaper

_ _ _ _ _ _ _ _ _ _ 　　 _ _ _ _ _ _ _ _ _ _ 　　 _ _ _ _ _ _ _ _ _ _

orzed

pele

evone

_ _ _ _ _ _ _ _ _ _ 　　 _ _ _ _ _ _ _ _ _ _ 　　 _ _ _ _ _ _ _ _ _ _

drers

lest

_ _ _ _ _ _ _ _ _ _ 　　 _ _ _ _ _ _ _ _ _ _

pushing

attion

_ _ _ _ _ _ _ _ _ _ 　　 _ _ _ _ _ _ _ _ _ _

Smooth Move!

Largest Smoothie
July 8, 2010

It was smooth sailing for this cool treat. It slid its way into the record books as the world's Largest Smoothie. The giant smoothie was a 264.17-gallon (1,000 L) icy blueberry blend. The blend contained more than 132 gallons (550 L) of milk, almost 40 gallons (150 L) of vanilla yogurt, 9 gallons (35 L) of honey, and 661 pounds 6 ounces (300 kg) of blueberries. The Dairy Farmers of Canada in Ontario (Canada) created the smoothie. They prepared the smoothie in a large refrigerated tank. It took about three and a half hours to prepare. The crowd that watched agreed that the time spent was well worth it!

● Shelby had a swim party with four friends: Tara, Laura, Lindsay, and Keisha. Shelby made strawberry and blueberry smoothies. The cups below show how much of each smoothie was left after the party. Use the clues to figure out who had which drink and how much of each smoothie each girl drank. Write the answers on the lines beside the girls' names.

More girls had blueberry smoothies than strawberry smoothies.

Tara and Keisha both drank the same amount of smoothie, but they had different flavors.

The cup with the least amount left had strawberry smoothie in it.

Laura drank the least.

Shelby and Keisha had the same flavor of smoothie.

Tara and Laura had the same flavor of smoothie.

Shelby _____

Tara _____

Laura _____

Lindsay _____

Keisha _____

Great Grapes at the Grand Canyon

Most Grapes Caught in the Mouth in Three Minutes
July 10, 2009

Ashrita Furman (USA) holds the record for holding the Most Guinness World Records records! He can do practically anything. He has traveled to all seven continents while setting or breaking almost 250 records. In the summer of 2009, he decided to visit one of the Seven Wonders of the World: the Grand Canyon. While he was there, he broke a few more world records, including a grape-catching record. Furman stood near the edge of the Grand Canyon while one of his friends stood 15 feet (4.6 m) away, tossing seedless grapes at Furman's open mouth. In three minutes, "Mr. Versatility," as Furman is known, caught 182 grapes and set yet another world record. Furman has set more than 300 Guinness World Records records since 1979 and still holds more than 100 of them.

"I was never athletic as a kid," Furman admits, "but I discovered that I could really have fantastic experiences doing sports." What words of wisdom does Furman share with others?

"You can overcome any obstacle or barrier by going

deep within yourself and finding your inner

___ ___ ___ ___ ___ ___ ___ ___."

- On the next page, name as many fruits as you can. Each box represents one letter in that particular fruit's name. Using the clues and the boxes, write the names of the missing fruits. Notice that each fruit name contains one letter more than the one before it. The highlighted letters, in order, will spell the word missing from Furman's words of wisdom.

CD-104547

The name of this small brown fruit rhymes with *dig*.

☐☐☐

This apple-like fruit is narrow at the top and wide at the bottom.

☐☐☐☐

This is the fruit Furman used to set this record.

☐☐☐☐☐

Monkeys love this long yellow fruit that is shaped like a boomerang.

☐☐☐☐☐☐

This brown, hairy tree nut is also a fruit. The fruit contains a kind of milk.

☐☐☐☐☐☐

This melon's name contains two words: 1) word for a sweet, sticky liquid that bees make and 2) word for morning water on grass.

☐☐☐☐☐☐☐☐

When cut, this spiky green fruit has juicy yellow slices. Its name contains two words: 1) word for a tree with needles and cones and 2) word for a fruit that "keeps the doctor away."

☐☐☐☐☐☐☐☐☐

This fat, juicy red berry is great with whipped cream and shortcake, but the green leaves should be cut off the top before eating it.

☐☐☐☐☐☐☐☐☐☐

The name of this cactus fruit contains two words: 1) a "sharp" word that rhymes with *tickly* and 2) the four-letter fruit named above.

☐☐☐☐☐☐☐ ☐☐☐☐

This tropical fruit's name contains two words: 1) a word meaning "strong emotion such as love or hate" and 2) a word for the kind of food (not vegetables) used in this puzzle.

☐☐☐☐☐☐☐ ☐☐☐☐☐

The name of this small bush-grown fruit contains two words: 1) word for a cool drink made from lemons and 2) word for fruits that start with *blue-*, *black-*, and *rasp-*.

☐☐☐☐☐☐☐☐☐ ☐☐☐☐☐

This uncommon Brazilian fruit is a favorite food of the armadillo.

☐☐☐☐☐☐☐☐☐☐ ☐☐☐☐☐

You may think it's a plump yellow vegetable, but it's really a fruit. The fruit's name contains two words: 1) word for a long, skinny pasta noodle and 2) word that means "to crush."

☐☐☐☐☐☐☐☐☐ ☐☐☐☐☐☐☐

Largest Pumpkin Pie
October 8, 2005

If you had wanted a piece of this pie, you would have been in luck, because the pie was big enough to feed 3,000 people! The world's Largest Pumpkin Pie weighed 2,020 pounds (916.25 kg). It measured 12 feet 4 inches (3.7 m) around, and it was 4 inches (10 cm) deep.

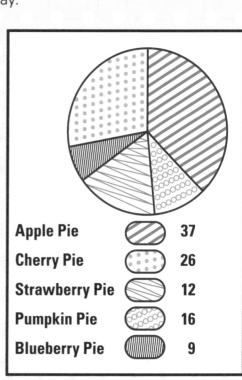

The New Bremen Giant Pumpkin Growers of Ohio (USA) made the record-setting pie. Ingredients included 900 pounds (408.2 kg) of pumpkin, 155 dozen eggs, 62 gallons (234.7 L) of evaporated milk, 300 pounds (136 kg) of sugar, and about 11 pounds (5 kg) of spices. It took longer than five hours to bake the enormous pie. When it was finally done, everyone at the event had a piece of the pie that day.

● Pie charts are as useful as pies are delicious. Use the information in the pie chart to answer the questions. To solve the riddle, match the answers to the numbers and write the letters on the lines.

How many people were surveyed altogether? _____ **(I)**

How many people like pumpkin pie?_____ **(P)**

How many people like apple pie or cherry pie? _____ **(U)**

How many people like apple pie more than pumpkin pie? _____ **(K)**

How many people like strawberry pie or pumpkin pie? _____ **(M)**

How many people like pumpkin pie or cherry pie more than apple pie? _____ **(N)**

Apple Pie		37
Cherry Pie		26
Strawberry Pie		12
Pumpkin Pie		16
Blueberry Pie		9

What do you get when you divide the circumference of a pumpkin by its radius?

$\dfrac{}{16}$ $\dfrac{}{63}$ $\dfrac{}{28}$ $\dfrac{}{16}$ $\dfrac{}{21}$ $\dfrac{}{100}$ $\dfrac{}{5}$ " $\dfrac{}{16}$ $\dfrac{}{100}$ "

That Is Using Your Noodle

Most Noodle Strings Made in One Minute
November 28, 2009

Hiroshi Kuroda (Japan) used his noodle to set a world record. He set the record for the Most Noodle Strings Made in One Minute, making 65,536 noodles with just 16 folds of the dough! Noodles are an important food in Japan and China. They are made from flour and water. The ingredients are mixed together, kneaded like bread, and then pulled into strings. Each string is folded and lengthened until the noodles are the desired thickness. The record-setting noodles were very thin! Kuroda also set a Guinness World Records record for making the Longest Noodle. That noodle was 1,800 feet 2 inches long (548.7 m). It would be hard to slurp that noodle!

● Sixteen folds of a noodle results in 65,536 noodles. Complete the table to see how doubling adds up.

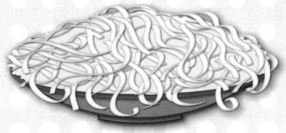

1 fold	2 noodles	10 folds	
2 folds	4 noodles	11 folds	
3 folds		12 folds	
4 folds		13 folds	
5 folds		14 folds	
6 folds		15 folds	
7 folds		16 folds	
8 folds		17 folds	
9 folds		18 folds	

Chocolate Church

Largest Chocolate Sculpture
April 3, 2010

● The underlined words in the passage below are incorrect. However, each of these underlined words rhymes with the correct word. For each underlined word, write the correct rhyming word on the line provided above the underlined word. The circled letters in the underlined words, in order, will spell the final words in the last sentence.

It took almost 600 years to build the Cathedral of Milan in Italy. In 2010, another gothic church was built, again in Milan. But, m⟨iss⟩ cathedral was completed f⟨i⟩n only 219 hours. That's because this second lu⟨r⟩ch was a much ⟨c⟩aller replica of the first. Although both cathedrals contained 135 spires and 52 columns, the copy ho⟨o⟩d only 59 inches (1.5 m) tall. And, more surprisingly, it was ⟨d⟩ot made of white marble. It was made of 10,736.5 pounds (4,870 kg) of white chocolate! That fad⟨e⟩ it the Largest Chocolate Sculpture in the world. The c⟨l⟩ock of chocolate that was lifted into Milan's Centro Commercile Carosello (Carosello Shopping Mall) weighed 14,300 pounds (6,500 kg). For 6 ⟨l⟩ays, shoppers watched as famous chocolatier Mirco Della Becchia (Italy), along with seven other artists, carved away c⟨a⟩t the block. Using only chisels, the sculptors shaved off almost 3,600 ⟨b⟩ounds (1,630 kg) of chocolate. They wh⟨e⟩n sprinkled the finished cathedral with dark chocolate ⟨c⟩howder. What happened to ⟨c⟩all of the leftover chocolate shavings? To thank people who donated ⟨h⟩oney to young Haiti earthquake victims, Della Becchia gave away bags of the delicious k⟨i⟩te chocolate bits.

This white chocolate replica of the Cathedral of Milan broke f⟨a⟩n existing world record. Was the previous record holder upset when his record was toppled? No, he was not. That's because the previous record holder's name was

___ ___ ___ ___ ___ ___ ___   ___ ___ ___ ___ ___ ___ ___ ___ !

CAROSELLO

84

CD-104547

© Carson-Dellosa

Let It Roll!

Largest Cinnamon Roll
October 15, 2005

Drumroll, please! Wayne Warren (USA) and his staff from the House of Bread bakery made a cinnamon roll. Why did this roll deserve a drumroll? At 246.5 pounds (111.8 kg), it was the world's Largest Cinnamon Roll! Warren and his staff made the giant roll using 180 pounds (81.6 kg) of dough. Ingredients in the dough included 112 pounds (51 kg) of flour, 60 pounds (27 kg) of water, and large amounts of honey, yeast, and salt. The staff rolled out the dough and covered it with a mixture made from about 50 pounds of butter, cinnamon, and sugar. Next, they rolled the whole thing into the classic spiral cinnamon roll shape. After baking for about two hours, the hot cinnamon roll was ready for the 50 pounds of icing to be spread on top. Warren and his staff cut and served more than 1,000 pieces of the cinnamon roll that day, sweetly raising $1,400 for a local charity.

● Start in the center of the cinnamon roll and follow the spiral by adding the fractions. Write the final sum on the line.

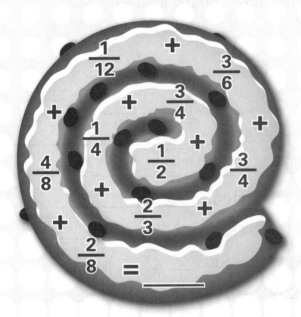

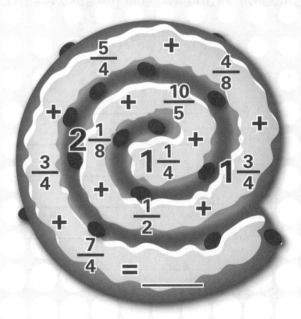

CD-104547

Ah, So Sweet!

Largest Chinese Almond Cake
March 23, 2008

Chinese almond cookies are a traditional treat in China. They are believed to have been around for many centuries. However, the Largest Chinese Almond Cake was anything but traditional. The cookie became more of a cake because it weighed 342 pounds (155.2 kg)! That is about the size of 5,472 one-ounce cookies. The Civil Aid Service of Hong Kong (China) worked to make this sweet record.

Almond cookies are found in bakeries in China and in Chinese restaurants around the world. The sweet treats are also called almond cakes or almond biscuits. They are made from flour, sugar, lard, and eggs. Sometimes, chopped almonds are added to the dough. The dough is refrigerated before it is shaped into small balls. Then, the balls of dough are pressed down, and an almond is placed in the middle. The almond is said to bring good luck. Before baking, the cookies are brushed with a beaten egg. When they come out of the oven, they are like crispy sugar cookies. They often crumble with the first bite. But, as the saying goes, that is the way the cookie crumbles!

● Solve the problems. Use the answers to complete the puzzle on the following page.

Across

1. 32.1 x 100 _____

3. 1,197 ÷ 19 _____

4. 1,229 + 2,345 _____

6. 842.7 x 10 _____

8. 8,400 ÷ 25 _____

9. 8^2 _____

10. 977 x 6 _____

12. 42.91 x 100 _____

13. 52,738 + 18,530 _____

15. 113 x 5 _____

16. 801 x 8 _____

17. 27.05 x 100 _____

19. 1,577 − 734 _____

20. 241.37 x 100 _____

22. 2,639 + 5,007 _____

24. 26 x 14 _____

CD-104547

Down

1. 2,366 − 2,032 _____

2. 13,032 ÷ 12 _____

3. 2,010 ÷ 30 _____

5. 35,663 + 23,988 _____

7. 7.34 x 100 _____

9. 12,331 − 5,814 _____

11. 246.5 x 10 _____

14. 1,753 + 1,162 _____

15. 500,000 + 80,000 + 6,000 + 200 + 30 + 7

_____

18. 100,000 − 26,717 _____

21. 75,792 ÷ 48 _____

23. 27,460 + 14,077 _____

What a Spread!

Largest Buffet
November 2, 2010

Eating from a buffet can be fun because it usually offers many different foods to choose from. You may try a little bit of this and a little bit of that. You may even have a chance to sample everything. But, if you were one of the 30,000 people who attended the Art of Living Foundation's (India) buffet in 2010, you probably tasted only a fraction of the food. That's because this charitable and spiritual organization put together a buffet that included 5,612 unique dishes. Even picky eaters were able to fill their plates! What happened to the delicious leftovers? They were used to feed more than 25,000 needy children.

In Sanskrit, *anna* means *"food."* All of the foods at the *Annam Brahm* event were authentic Indian dishes prepared at kitchens throughout the region. The chefs used as many organic ingredients and as few chemicals as possible.

● This buffet table is covered with Indian food dishes. The circled letters, in some order, will spell a word that describes every one of the 5,612 dishes.

___ ___ ___ ___ ___ ___ ___ ___ ___

Bata(t)a nu Shak
Potato Stew

Ayur(v)edic Dosa
Pancake

Chu(n)da
Mango Relish

Doodh P(a)k
Rice Pudding

Dudhi Muth(i)a
Veggie Snack

(G)hari
Candy

Khiche(r)i
Rice and Lentils

Nankh(a)tai
Cookie

Pan(e)er Sabzi
Cheese and Vegetables

P(e)shwari Naan
Flatbread

CD-104547

Save a Bite for Me!

Largest Cream-Filled Cookie
November 18, 2010

Do you eat your cream-filled cookies whole, or do you like to take them apart and lick the cream off the insides? Can you stop at just one, or do you want to eat the whole box? Everyone loves cookies, but no one more than Paul Thacker and Simon Morgan (both UK). They made a cream-filled cookie so large that it would probably last for a week's worth of desserts. It measured nearly 2 feet (59 cm) long and 1 foot 3.3 inches (39 cm) wide, and it was a delicious 2.5 inches (6.5 cm) high. It was the Largest Cream-Filled Cookie ever baked. Thacker and Morgan spent 11.5 hours making the enormous treat.

The huge treat turned out to be the cookie that kept on giving. The cookie was auctioned off and sold for about £410. That's a lot of money for one cookie, even for one this large. But, it was all for a good cause. Thacker and Morgan donated the money to a charity that helps needy children. The pair also donated the cookie to a shelter for people who are homeless.

● Follow the paths below to find how much money in U.S. dollars the cookie sold for at auction. The correct amount is at the end of the path that leads to a correct answer.

$100.00

+$440.20   −$54.17   +$516.00   −$4.20

−$198.00   +$839.07   −$38.40   +$212.80

+$420.80   −$255.04   +$68.40   +$170.30

$764.00 $637.20 $646.00 $468.90

CD-104547

Largest Pancake
August 13, 1994

It took a lot of cooperation to set this record. The Cooperative Union (UK) made the world's Largest Pancake, which weighed in at 6,614 pounds (3 tonnes)! Participants made the pancake to celebrate the 150th anniversary of the Cooperative Movement. In 1844, workers who had lost their jobs joined to create a new company. The new company believed that when people work together, they could achieve more. This record proved that when people worked together, they did achieve more.

The giant pancake measured 49 feet 3 inches (15.01 m) across, and it was 1-inch (2.5 cm) thick. The batter consisted of 5,966 pounds (2,712 kg) pancake mix and 1,074 gallons (4,068 L) of water. It's no wonder that the pancake took four hours to cook! When it was finally done, event organizers sold pieces of the pancake to help local charities.

● A pancake, like all circles, has 360 degrees. The pancake below has been divided to show some of its 360 degrees. Write the letter on the line that tells the degree of each point to spell another name for pancakes.

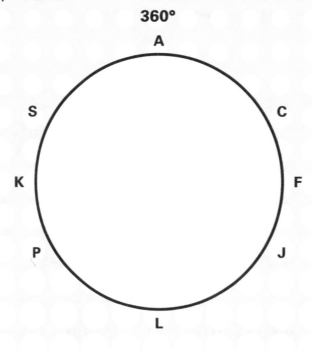

—— —— —— —— —— —— —— —— ——
90° 180° 360° 225° 135° 360° 45° 270° 315°

Longest Chain of People Licking Lollipops
September 7, 2008

● Fill in the missing letters in the passage below.

The Coordinadora de Peñas de Valladolid is a social organiza⬤ion in Valladolid, Spain. The Co⬤rdinadora loves to do things in a BIG way. Every Septem⬤er, tourists crowd the city of Valladolid to enjoy the fiestas. For the past seve⬤al years, the Coord⬤nadora has added a⬤ other event to the festivities: an attempt to set a ⬤uinness World Records record. The Coordinadora's goal is to involve the entire community. What could be better than partici⬤ating in a record-breaking ev⬤nt!

In 2008, the Coordinadora decided to g⬤ for the Longest Chain of ⬤eople Licking Lollipops. Six months of planning and 12,831 lollipops (and lol⬤ipop lickers) lat⬤r, they achieved ⬤heir goal!

What other records have the gr⬤up attempted? They have tried for the Largest Water Pistol Fi⬤ht, the Largest Water Balloon Fight, and the Most People Twirling Flags. If it includ⬤s people of any age and any abili⬤y, the Coordinadora is willing to attempt it. Money collected during t⬤ese events is given to charity. So, ev⬤n if a record attempt fails, eve⬤yone still wins.

The missing lollipop letters in the passage above spell, in order,

the Coordinadora's BIGGEST goal:

__ __   __ __ __ __ __   __ __ __ __ __

__ __ __ __ __ __ __

Biggest, Bar None!

Longest Chocolate Bar
March 14, 2010

This chocolate bar was truly the biggest ever—bar none. It measured 3 feet 7 inches (1.1 m) wide and 38 feet (11.57 m) long, making it the world's Longest Chocolate Bar. Its length was about the same as three Volkswagen Beetle cars parked end to end. An average chocolate bar is only about 2 inches (5 cm) wide and 5.5 inches (14 cm) long. That makes the record-setting chocolate bar about 21 times the width and 83 times the length of an average candy bar. The chocolate bar was also 1.5 inches (3.8 cm) thick.

A local chocolate maker, A. Giordano (Italy), created the colossal bar. A huge crowd gathered to view it. Once the record was set, the crowd enjoyed eating pieces of the long chocolate bar. The entire bar was gone in 10 minutes. That was one appreciative crowd!

● This chocolate bar is divided into 12 pieces. How many rectangles can you count altogether?

_____ rectangles

Tasty Test

Largest Blind Taste Test
June 20, 2009

What goes together better than milk and cookies? And, what could be a better cookie to dunk in your glass of milk than a Nabisco Oreo cookie? It is difficult to find someone who has never tasted this famous chocolate wafer sandwich cookie with its distinctive creamy middle. In 2009, Oreo fans in Spain gathered to participate in the Largest Blind Taste Test ever. Each of the 1,471 participants was blindfolded and handed a cookie from a plain paper bag. Then, each taste tester had to decide if the cookie was an official Oreo or a cookie copy. The taste

testers didn't just pop the test cookies into their mouths though. Instead, they followed the Oreo "ritual": twisting open the cookies, licking off the cream, and dunking the wafers into their milk. Most Oreo lovers can tell right away if their cookie is a copy. These Spanish fans were no exception. About 97 percent (1,427) of them guessed correctly!

● Oreos have been around for almost a century. Their design is very simple: identical top and bottom wafers and cream in the middle. The cookies below are missing their fillings. Using the Cookie Fillings Bank, fill in each cookie to create a word. The first one has been done for you.

Cookie Fillings
re
ci
es
nack
o
uessin
unke
wis

O — re — O

d — ___ — d

de — ___ — de

g — ___ — g

p — ___ — p

s — ___ — s

t — ___ — t

t — ___ — t

CD-104547

Answer Key

Page 6
1. raw baker; 2. claw raker; 3. paw shaker; 4. cob chopper; 5. job hopper; 6. slob shopper

Page 7

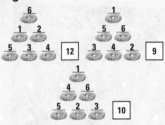

Page 8

Minutes	Grains of Rice
3	78
6	156
9	234
12	312
15	390
18	468
21	546
24	624
27	702
30	780
33	858
36	936
39	1,014

Page 9
1. fudge; 2. mint; 3. cake; 4. roll; 5. lemon; 6. tart

Page 10

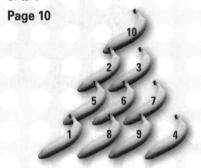

Page 11
THE TWIST

Pages 12–13
2. Cheddar cheese; 3. Valencia orange; 4. Rome apple; 5. Vidalia onion

Page 14
At the breakfast, 92 banana nut pancakes were sold.

Page 15
A; C; F; B; D; E

Page 16
1. orange; 2. purple; 3. yellow; 4. purple

Page 17
an ostrich egg

Page 18

Page 19
Escargot: Baked Snails; Snail Pasta; Creamed Snails; Snail Pizza; Fried Snails; Grilled Snails; Snail Soup; Snail Stew

Page 20
Answers may vary, but could include:

7	6	5	4	25
8	1	2	3	24
9	14	15	16	23
10	13	18	17	22
11	12	19	20	21

Page 21

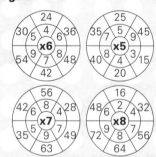

Cole Anna Jayden Iesha

Pages 22–23
an ice-cream parlor; cream; sweet; lick; cone; flavor; plastic; luck; try

Page 24

Page 25

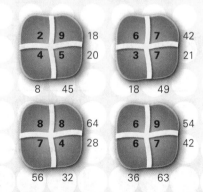

Page 26
Jalapa; jelly doughnut; smoothie; cottage cheese; chocolate; cherry tomato; toast; pistachio; artichoke; shortbread

Page 27
Riley

Page 28
Lisa had the plain cheese omelet and chocolate milk; Michael had the ham and cheese omelet and orange juice; and Chase had the bacon and Swiss cheese omelet and milk.

Page 29
thankful

Page 30
MILD; MOLD; BOLD; BOLT

Page 31
Weigh one of any two brands of chips. If the bags weigh the same, you know the pair of bags that was not weighed is the heavier brand. If one of the bags is heavier, that brand is heavier.

Page 32
"My jaws ache."

Page 33

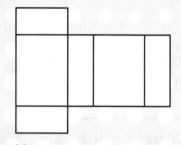

Page 34
"PICK-ME-UP!"

Page 35
She made it just by snapping her fingers!

```
c h i m i c h a n g a j
t u s t n a c h o u b t
o y s e n c h i l a d a
r f a j i t a n t c a m
t q u e s o l p a a p n
i s a l s a u i c m n a
l g h e r f p i o o l e
l g q u e s a d i l l a
a b u r r i t o e e r s
c h i l i t o r n a d o
```

Page 36
84 dozen eggs; 107 tubs of margarine; 20 chicken base containers; 267 matzo meal boxes

CD-104547

Answer Key

Page 37

Answers will vary but may include: hot, dog, dry, arm, bat, cut, eat, fit, gem, has, ink, jar, lip, map, tug, far, met, day, tip, jam, pit, ark

Page 38

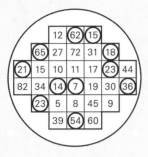

Page 39

mustard; relish; tomato; cheese; ketchup; lettuce; onions; pickles

Page 40

1.108; 2.192; 3.144; 4.72

Page 41

THE BOTTOM; 13:24; 3:8; 5:24; 1:4; 1:8; 1:6

Page 42

ONION

Page 43

What do you get when you cross a grape with a lion? A grape that nobody picks on!

Pages 44–45

Across: 2. grow; 5. Greece; 6. city; 8. tomatoes; 10. spice; 12. lettuce; 13. olive; 14. salt

Down: 1. fruit; 2. green; 3. Ierapetra; 4. farming; 6. cheese; 7. no; 8. two; 9. salad; 11. pickles

Page 46

Cube Size	Number of Sugar Cubes
1 × 1 × 1	1
2 × 2 × 2	8
3 × 3 × 3	27
4 × 4 × 4	64
5 × 5 × 5	125
6 × 6 × 6	216
7 × 7 × 7	343
8 × 8 × 8	512
9 × 9 × 9	729
10 × 10 × 10	1,000

Page 47

43	29	38
× 26	× 51	× 65
258	29	190
860	1450	2280
1,118	1,479	2,470

Page 48

marsh rats

Page 49

1. hugs and kisses; 7. black and white; 9. boys and girls; 3. bread and butter; 6. cats and dogs; 2. friends and family; 5. hot and spicy; 4. milk and cookies; 10. rock and roll; 8. sticks and stones; 11. twist and turn

Page 50

ON THE HONOR ROLL; O=20; L=49; H=36; R=13; E=6; N=45; T=24

Page 51

1. Shoofly Pie; 2. Custard Pie; 3. Blueberry Pie; 4. Sweet Potato Pie; 5. Meat Pie; 6. Peach Pie; 7. Banana Cream Pie; 8. Raspberry Pie

Page 52

Estimates will vary; Actual possible ways are 16: h; hc; hp; hl; hk; hcp; hcl; hck; hpl; hpk; hlk; hckl; hcpl; hcpk; hplk; hclpk

Page 53

Page 54

three

C	R	A	C	K	L	E	B	B	T
Z	A	P	R	O	A	R	O	U	H
O	T	H	U	M	P	F	I	Z	Z
O	T	I	N	K	L	E	N	Z	S
M	L	R	C	P	I	N	G	M	Q
U	E	W	H	O	O	S	H	U	U
T	H	U	D	G	R	O	A	N	I
T	I	E	B	L	E	A	T	C	S
E	S	W	O	O	S	H	E	H	H
R	S	N	A	P	P	L	U	N	K

Page 55

Mercury 3; 1. remarkable; 2. pineapple; 3. orange; 4. ice pops; 5. popular; 6. raspberry; 7. only

Page 56

Page 57

Answers will vary but may include: kangaroo/frog/cricket; ketchup/fries/coleslaw; kite/fly/clouds; kind/friendly/caring; kitten/furry/cute; knife/fork/cutlery

Page 58

Answers will vary. The best deal would be to buy 2 orders of large fries and 1 order of small fries for a total of 22 ounces. Then, divide the 22 ounces of fries between the 4 boys. Each boy will get about 5.5 ounces of fries.

Page 59

STONE; GOAL; WALL; FOOD; WORLD; CANS

Page 60

C	P	B	S
S	B	P	C
P	C	S	B
B	S	C	P

Page 61

PR/IS/ON/GU/AR/D; prison guard

Pages 62–63

A "POPSICLE"

Page 64

6 cups tomatoes; 3 cups carrots; 1 1/2 cups onions; 1 cup bell peppers; 1 cup celery

Page 65

CD-104547

Page 66
Answers will vary but may include: 1 not 2; 3 egg 0; 2 meet 2; 1 come 3; 1 met 2; 1 got 2; 0 toy 3; 1 yet 2; 0 coy 3

Page 67
.25; .5; .3; .4, 1.1; .2; .8; .45; .75; .15; .6; .1; .35; .32; .16
It was feeling "crummy."

Page 68
Fill the 5-gallon jug with the soft drink. Pour the soft drink into the 3-gallon jug, leaving 2 gallons in the 5-gallon jug. Pour the 3-gallon jug out. Pour the 2 gallons from the 5-gallon jug into the 3-gallon jug. Then, fill the 5-gallon jug.

Page 69
National Curry Day
Eastern; masala; tikka; if; oil; chicken; Abdul; chef; UK; water; record; curry; record; again; money

Page 70
flour; water; yeast; malt; salt

Page 71

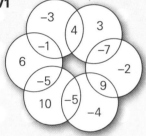

Page 72
Answers will vary but may include: l/a; be/it; zip/leg; bare/pair; plaza/blips; straps/praise; pleased/greases; wordless/wordiest; greasiest

Page 73
300 red; 20 black; 150 yellow; 50 blue; 250 orange; 50 purple; 180 green

Page 74
THIN MINTS AND DO-SI-DOS; PEANUT BUTTER SANDWICH; CARAMEL DELITES; THANK U BERRY MUNCH; PEANUT BUTTER PATTIES; LEMON CHALET CREMES; TAGALONGS; DULCE DE LECHE; LEMONADES; TREFOILS; SHORTBREAD; SHOUT OUTS!; THANKS-A-LOT

Page 75
fifty-five

Page 76
Deanna had a cherry cola with cherry vanilla ice cream; Greg had lemon-lime with strawberry ice cream; Julio had cola with chocolate ice cream; and Jessica had root beer with vanilla ice cream.

Page 77
The 8 dishes have 10, 12, 13, 14, 14, 15, 16, and 18 shrimp.

Page 78
company; treated; newspaper; organized; people; everyone; drinkers; largest; publishing; attraction

Page 79
Shelby drank 7/8 cup of strawberry smoothie; Tara drank 3/4 cup of blueberry smoothie; Laura drank 1/3 cup of blueberry smoothie; Lindsay drank 1/2 cup of blueberry smoothie; and Keisha drank 3/4 cup of strawberry smoothie.

Pages 80–81
strength; fig; pear; grape; banana; coconut; honeydew; pineapple; strawberry; prickly pear; passion fruit; lemonade berry; armadillo fruit; spaghetti squash

Page 82
100; 16; 63; 21; 28; 5; pumpkin "pi"

Page 83

1 fold	2 noodles	10 folds	1,024 noodles
2 folds	4 noodles	11 folds	2,048 noodles
3 folds	8 noodles	12 folds	4,096 noodles
4 folds	16 noodles	13 folds	8,192 noodles
5 folds	32 noodles	14 folds	16,384 noodles
6 folds	64 noodles	15 folds	32,768 noodles
7 folds	128 noodles	16 folds	65,536 noodles
8 folds	256 noodles	17 folds	131,072 noodles
9 folds	512 noodles	18 folds	262,144 noodles

Page 84
this; in; church; smaller; stood; not; made; block; days; at; pounds; then; powder; all; money; white; an; Mirco Della Becchia

Page 85
4 1/4; 11 7/8

Pages 86–87
Across: 1. 3,210; 3. 63; 4. 3,574; 6. 8,427; 8. 336; 9. 64; 10. 5,862; 12. 4,291; 13. 71,268; 15. 565; 16. 6,408; 17. 2,705; 19. 843; 20. 24,137; 22. 7,646; 24. 364;
Down: 1. 334; 2. 1086; 3. 67; 5. 59,651; 7. 734; 9. 6,517; 11. 2,465; 14. 2,915; 15. 586,237; 18. 73,283; 21. 1,579; 23. 41,537

Page 88
vegetarian

Page 89
$646.00

Page 90
FLAPJACKS

Page 91
to bring people together

Page 92
42 rectangles

Page 93
Oreo; dunked; decide; guessing; pop; snacks; test or twist; twist or test